By Jim Ladd

40 DAYS | 40 BIBLICAL TRUTHS

Evergreen Christian Community
1000 Black Lake Blvd.
Olympia WA 98502

Scriptures taken from the Holy Bible, New International Version, 2011 (Zondervan).
Used by permission.

TABLE OF
CONTENTS

A NOTE FROM
PASTOR JIM LADD

"You have formed us for Yourself, and our hearts are restless until they find their rest in You." - St. Augustine

It is my dream and delight to help people find and follow Jesus. My hope is that your journey through *The Pursuit* will help you to do exactly that. During this 40-day discussion, my goal is for you to learn 40 Biblical Truths, memorize eight verses of Scripture, and have eight faith-shaping conversations. These Truths are foundational to your lifelong pursuit of knowing God, experiencing His love, and living your life on mission with Him. Because our faith is continually being shaped by our relationships, these eight conversations will help you anchor your faith in Christ.

The 40 Truths we will explore together are the rich Biblical and theological tenets of the Christian faith, which we rarely have time on Sunday mornings to adequately investigate. The purpose of *The Pursuit* is not apologetics of Christian doctrine, and it is not made to explain *why* we believe, but rather to explore *what* we believe. Through this systematic view of Biblical Christian faith, I believe you will move forward in knowing and walking with God, understanding His ways, and seeing your place in His eternal story.

I humbly ask that you make a few commitments as you begin:

- » Aim for doing the daily work five days a week for the whole eight weeks.
- » Do not take this journey alone! Meet weekly to do the eight conversations with a friend, with another couple if you're married, or with a group of friends.
- » Try and have the group discussions for every one of the eight weeks, but don't settle for less than six. If you miss one or two, still do the daily work on those weeks so that your personal journey can continue to make progress.
- » Make an extraordinary commitment to this two-month season of your life.

I am so excited that you have decided to draw on this resource as part of your journey. I know the Holy Spirit will meet you, challenge you, and encourage you over the next eight weeks. May you joyfully lean into Jesus and discover that He is nearer, wilder, and more wonderful than you have ever imagined. May His Presence in your life foster a peace that surpasses your mental comprehension.

I also want to give special recognition and appreciation to my son, Jonathan Ladd, who helped me write and edit *The Pursuit*. What an honor it was to work with him on this project.

Let *the pursuit* begin!

Jim Ladd

SERIES OVERVIEW

SERIES DESCRIPTION

Each week begins with an introduction to the topic of conversation and a memory verse for the week. This is followed by five daily devotional reflections, each on a Truth that feeds that week's overall topic. These daily devotions will require about 10 minutes of your day. The week ends with a small group discussion guide to help you and your group to sharpen your grasp on the Truths being studied. After the eight weeks, there is a page for you to plan the next steps of your spiritual formation process and continue the journey.

CONVERSATION 1 WHO IS GOD?
≋ *Memory Verse: 2 Samuel 7:22*

Truth #1 God is the Sovereign Creator
Truth #2 God is the Comprehensive Sustainer of All things
Truth #3 He is One God Existing in Three Persons
Truth #4 God is Merciful and Just
Truth #5 God is with Us

CONVERSATION 2 WHAT IS MAN?
≋ *Memory Verse: 1 John 3:1*

Truth #6 Man is an Image Bearer
Truth #7 Man has Rebelled Against God
Truth #8 Man is Utterly Depraved
Truth #9 Man is the Central Object of God's Affection
Truth #10 Man was Made to Glorify God

CONVERSATION 3 **WHAT DOES GOD REQUIRE OF US?**

Memory Verse: Mark 12:30-31

Truth #11 God's Law is Stated in the 10 Commandments
Truth #12 Nobody Can Keep God's Law Perfectly
Truth #13 The Purpose of the Law is to Show Us Our Sin
Truth #14 Sin is Lawlessness
Truth #15 Jesus Satisfies the Law of God

CONVERSATION 4 **WHO IS JESUS?**

Memory Verse: Hebrews 4:14

Truth #16 Jesus is the Hero of All Creation
Truth #17 Jesus is the Exact Representation of God's Nature
Truth #18 Jesus is the Mediator between God and Man
Truth #19 Jesus is God, Redeeming Man Back to Himself
Truth #20 Jesus was Fully Human

CONVERSATION 5 **WHAT IS THE GOSPEL?**

Memory Verse: 2 Timothy 1:9

Truth #21 All of Our Sins can be Forgiven
Truth #22 Jesus Reconciles All Things
Truth #23 The Grace of Jesus is Offered to All People
Truth #24 We are Saved by Grace Through Faith
Truth #25 We are Justified and are Being Sanctified

CONVERSATION 6 **HOW DOES GOD CONTINUE TO WORK IN ME?**

Memory Verse: 2 Corinthians 5:17

Truth #26 I am Baptized Into the Body of Christ
Truth #27 I Am Occupied by the Holy Spirit
Truth #28 I Must Participate in My Ongoing Transformation
Truth #29 I Was Made for a Mission
Truth #30 I Can Enjoy Eternal Life Today

CONVERSATION 7 **WHAT IS THE CHURCH?**

☰ *Memory Verse: Ephesians 3:10-11*

Truth #31 We are the Called-Out Ones
Truth #32 We are the People of God's Presence
Truth #33 We are Citizens of God's Kingdom
Truth #34 We are a Prophetic Voice to the Culture
Truth #35 We Serve One Objective - The Glory of God

CONVERSATION 8 **HOW IS IT ALL GOING TO END?**

☰ *Memory Verse: Revelation 21:1-2*

Truth #36 Christ will Return Again, in Victory
Truth #37 Every Person Will Give an Account to God
Truth #38 Hell is the Eternal Home for Those who Reject God
Truth #39 Heaven is Prepared for The Redeemed
Truth #40 There Will be a New Heaven and a New Earth

CONVERSATION 1
WHO IS GOD?

WEEK 1 INTRODUCTION

Every one of us, no matter our history, context, or experience, has some idea of what we think about God. Is He real? Does He exist? Did He create everything and then disappear, or does He remain involved in creation and participate in it? For some, He is the Great Judge waiting to strike them dead if they get out of bounds. For others, He is the cosmic Santa Claus or emergency response team - ready to respond with gifts or rescue when called upon. Still for others He is the cruel, negligent, and unworthy One who is to blame for the disaster that has become the human world.

The problem is that none of our ideas can be entirely accurate, for He is so far above and beyond our capacity to understand that our images and words cannot adequately capture Him. We cannot fully grasp, nor therefore describe, His majesty, glory, endlessness, and power. Our three pounds of human brain simply cannot comprehend the depth and breadth of God. Therefore, God must reveal Himself to us if we are to know Him with any accuracy at all.

WEEK 1 MEMORY VERSE

"How great you are, Sovereign Lord! There is no one like you, and there is no God but you..."

2 Samuel 7:22

TRUTH #1
GOD IS THE SOVEREIGN CREATOR

QUOTE

"Just because somebody uses the word God and then somebody else uses the word God, it does not follow that they mean the same thing. God, for some, is an inexpressible feeling, or it is the unmoved cause at the beginning of the universe, or it is a being full of transcendence. But we are talking about the God of the Bible, and the God of the Bible is self-defined. He talks about himself as being eternal and righteous. He is the God of love. He is the God of transcendence; that is, he is above space and time and history. Yet he is the immanent God; that is, he is so much with us that we cannot possibly escape from him. He is everywhere. He is unchangeable. He is truthful. He is reliable. He is personal."
- D. A. Carson

SCRIPTURE

"In the beginning, God..."
- Genesis 1:1

DEVOTIONAL

The first four words of the Bible give us all the information we need to understand our position in the universe. From these four simple words we can immediately recognize that life comes *from* God, is found *in* God, and exists *for* God. He who was the beginning and source of all things naturally has the authority to govern our existence.

However difficult this may be for our rebellious hearts to accept, it is unalterably true. Like the Priest in the movie, "Rudy," if we only know two things, they are the two things that guide us best: "There is a God and I am not Him."

The history of the world is the ongoing story of man's dogged insistence that it is he who is sovereign, not God. Man is the perpetual toddler, stuck in the "terrible twos" and continues to stomp his feet, raise his voice, and scream, "Mine!" to God. But it is the Creator who gets to form the creation any way He desires. The

Creator makes the rules, sets the limitations, and determines the outcomes for His creation.

> "*The Creator of the world is doubtless also the Governor of it. He that had power to give being to the world, and set all the parts of it in order, has doubtless power to dispose of the world, to continue the order he has constituted, or to alter it. He that first gave the laws of nature, must have all nature in his hands. So it is evident God has the world in his hands, to dispose of as he pleases.*"
> **- Jonathan Edwards**

God has decided to allow His created ones to choose who they trust: their creator or themselves. But our decision in this regard does not affect God or His Sovereign plans, for He already knows the decisions we will make and will use both our obedience and our rebellion to accomplish His sovereign will.

Yes, there is a Sovereign One and you are not Him.

PRAYER

Holy God, the Creator and Lord of all things, everything exists because of your will. The smallest creature is known to you and the greatest nation is at your command. Your rule cannot be stopped and your will shall be accomplished. Help me trust you and your goodness in all things. Amen.

REFLECTION QUESTIONS

 » Does the idea of God's Sovereignty comfort you or confront you? Or both?
 » What are three ways you might demonstrate complete submission to God's authority in your life?
 » No matter whether you choose submission or rebellion, God knows it in advance and will use it to further His sovereign will. How do you feel about that?
 » Practice this week's memory verse.

TRUTH #2
GOD IS THE COMPREHENSIVE SUSTAINER OF ALL THINGS

QUOTE

"There's only one power in the world great enough to help us rise above the difficult things we face: the power of God."
- Stormie Omartian

SCRIPTURE

"Through him and for him all things were made; without him nothing was made that has been made. In him was life, and that life was the light of all mankind."
- John 1:2-4

DEVOTIONAL

God exists outside of time and He created all things out of nothing. The heavens declare His glory and the earth reveals His Majesty. He is in everything and exists everywhere, but His creation cannot contain Him. His Presence gives life and life cannot exist without Him.

The Apostle Paul described him this way, "The God who made the world and everything in it is the Lord of heaven and earth and does not live in temples built by human hands... he himself gives everyone life and breath and everything else. From one man he made all the nations, that they should inhabit the whole earth; and he marked out their appointed times in history and the boundaries of their lands. God did this so that they would seek him and perhaps reach out for him and find him, though he is not far from any one of us. 'For in him we live and move and have our being.'" (Acts 17:24-28)

God is present and active in every aspect of Creation, maintaining the order of all things even in our fallen world. And God has made a way for us to experience life in His Kingdom, all day every day, through the death and resurrection of Jesus. "The Son is the image of the invisible God, the firstborn over all creation. For in Him all things were created: things in heaven and on earth, visible and invisible, whether thrones or powers or rulers or authorities; all things have been created through Him and for Him. He is before all things, and in Him all things hold together." (Colossians 1:15-17)

Therefore we will not be afraid, even when the earth gives way and the mountains fall into the sea. Instead, we fix our thoughts on Jesus, our apostle and high priest; the initiator and sustainer of our faith, who will never leave us or forsake us.

PRAYER

Lord who spoke the world into existence, I am in awe of You. I marvel at Your creation and see Your beauty in the splendor of the stars. Your might is shown forth in the strength of a hurricane. Your order is displayed in the laws of mathematics. Let everything that has breath praise the Lord for the works and sustaining power of Your hands! Amen.

REFLECTION QUESTIONS

- » Where are you when you feel the closest to God? (practice that today)
- » Do you have a tendency to tell God how big your problems are, or to tell your problems how big God is? Why?
- » If God was to speak to your current fears or anxieties, what would He say? (take a few moments to listen for His answer)
- » Practice this week's memory verse.

TRUTH #3
HE IS ONE GOD EXISTING IN THREE PERSONS

QUOTE

"It is commonly said that the Trinity is a mystery. And it certainly is ... But it is not a mystery veiled in darkness in which we can only grope and guess. It is a mystery in which we understand that we will never know all there is of God ... It is not a mystery that keeps us in the dark, but a mystery in which we are taken by the hand and gradually led into the light. "
- Eugene Peterson

SCRIPTURE

"The grace of the Lord Jesus Christ and the love of God and the fellowship of the Holy Spirit be with you all."
- 2 Corinthians 13:14

DEVOTIONAL

The word "Trinity" is never found in Scripture, yet it is one of the most helpful theological principles to understand. That God has chosen to reveal Himself to us as One God in three Persons is clear, and it is great news for us that He has. Seeing the triune God helps us to better understand the nature of who He is, the depth of His commitment to us, and the transformational future He makes available to us.

God is One and there is no other. The Father is God; the Son is God; the Holy Spirit is God. Even more clearly, the Father is not the Son; the Son is not the Spirit; and the Spirit is not the Father. They are equal and have coexisted for eternity. Like a prism held to the light, we see new colors of the majesty and beauty of God as we examine Him in each of these ways.

God is the Father of all creation, who possesses sovereign power. God is the Son who self-sacrificially participates in our world. And God is the Spirit whose ever-abiding Presence works with us to the end.

Understanding His triune nature helps us to experience His radical love and to see His redemptive commitment to us more vividly. God the Father made us, God the Son suffered violently for our rebellion, and God the Spirit enables us to taste now the glory that we will one day enjoy forever without limit.

As the triune God, He is your Father, who freely gives you all good things. He is your elder brother who makes a way for the Father to welcome you home from the disaster of your foolish rebellion. And He is your counselor, who nurtures you toward the wholeness and life the Father had in mind when He made you. Each Person of the Trinity uniquely helps us to know God and His great work in us.

> *"Oh, the depth of the riches of the wisdom and knowledge of God! How unsearchable his judgments, and his paths beyond tracing out! To him be the glory forever! Amen."*
> **- Romans 11:33**

PRAYER

Oh God, the Father, Son and Spirit, you are beyond my understanding. Thank you for revealing yourself to me and bringing me into your love. Help me to know you more and to grow in loving you like you love me. Amen.

REFLECTION QUESTIONS

- » Why do you think God chose to reveal Himself to us in three Persons?
- » How is knowing God as Father helpful to you? How is it difficult for you?
- » Take a moment and give a sentence of praise to God the Father, God the Son and God the Holy Spirit.
- » Practice this week's memory verse.

TRUTH #4
GOD IS MERCIFUL AND JUST

QUOTE

"Mercy, detached from Justice, grows unmerciful."
- C. S. Lewis

SCRIPTURE

"For God did not send His Son into the world to condemn the world, but that the world might have life in His Name."
- John 3:17

DEVOTIONAL

One day my hero, Moses, after walking faithfully with God for a long time, asked God to show him His glory. It was a bold request, for sure, and God decided to satisfy it. So, in Exodus 34, He passed in front of Moses, proclaiming, "The Lord, the Lord, the compassionate and gracious God, slow to anger, abounding in love and faithfulness, maintaining love to thousands, and forgiving wickedness, rebellion and sin. Yet He does not leave the guilty unpunished" (Exodus 34:6,7). Moses bowed to the ground at once and worshiped.

Wise man.

It is God's glory that He is both merciful and just. This may at first sound like a paradox, as it seems in life that justice and mercy are at odds with each other, and one should be unable to give both. Yet God shows that there is one way to give both at the same time: while justice demands that the penalty be paid, mercy allows the innocent to pay it. The wages of sin is death and no sin will go unpunished, but it is the mercy of God that He made a way for the guilty to live. God in the person of Jesus, who knew no sin, became sin, that we might receive the mercy of God. It is the glory of God to show mercy without compromising justice.

This charge occurs 41 times in the Bible: "Give thanks to the Lord, for He is good; *His love endures forever*." And so does His justice. The author of Hebrews urges us to give our all to God and warns us that "it is a dreadful thing to fall into the hands of the living God."

God's justice confronts the wickedness of our hearts while His mercy invites us to find our new selves in Christ, who paid the penalty for our injustice.

God is not mocked - one day we will all stand before His judgment seat and be forced to give a defense for our actions. On that day, any defense we offer that is not a complete and utter reliance on the shed, holy blood of Jesus will fail. This is the great mercy of a God who is perfectly just. And the best way to prepare for that day of judgment is to bow and confess Christ today and everyday.

PRAYER

Just and merciful Father, when I am covered in the righteousness of Christ, you remember my sins no more. You have thrown them as far as the east is from the west and cast them into the sea of forgetfulness. Help me to not doubt your forgiveness, your mercy, or your love, but to come to you boldly as your beloved child. Amen.

REFLECTION QUESTIONS

- » Usually, we want justice for others and mercy for ourselves. Reflect on what it would be like to desire mercy for everyone.
- » If God offers mercy to everyone, how is justice served?
- » Scripture says that if we confess our sin, God is faithful and just to forgive them. How deeply do you believe this? What is it like to stake your life on this?
- » Practice this week's memory verse.

TRUTH #5
GOD IS WITH US

QUOTE

"The Presence of God is the central fact of Christianity. At the heart of the Christian message is God Himself waiting for His redeemed children to push into conscious awareness of His Presence."
- Jonathan Edwards

SCRIPTURE

"The Lord himself goes before you and will be with you; he will never leave you nor forsake you. Do not be afraid; do not be discouraged."
- Deuteronomy 31:8

DEVOTIONAL

In his final study session with the disciples, before the cross, Jesus told them that his imminent departure was actually a good thing for them. He told them that the Father would then send them another Comforter - the Spirit of God. He said that the world cannot accept or understand Him, but that the Spirit would be with them and *in* them. "On that day you will realize that I am in my Father, and you are in me and I am in you." (John 14:20). This was an astounding promise for us all.

Then, when the time finally came for Jesus to ascend to the Father, He told the disciples to anticipate the promised arrival of the Holy Spirit and to expect that the Presence and Power of God would be their new normal. He used the Greek word *dunamis* to describe that power, which you may recognize as the root word for an explosive device that can move mountains (dynamite). And such is His Presence and Power in the Person of the Holy Spirit in us.

The coming of the Holy Spirit and His availability to all mankind is not a small footnote in the grand story of God. It accompanies the sacrifice of Jesus as a declaration of war on sin and the forces of evil. At the moment Jesus took his last breath on the cross, the veil of the temple was completely torn in two. On the other side of that veil was the altar, where only the High Priest would encounter the Presence of God, and only the High Priest could enter. With the death of Jesus,

God destroyed the barrier between ourselves and Him, and invited every one of us into a personal relationship with Him. Now the Presence of God is available to all people!

Hey, God is with you.

Can a more significant thing ever be said of anyone? He is with you; His victory is yours; His Power is yours; nothing shall be impossible for you. His Presence and Power are yours and mine so that we might bear witness in the world to the reality of His grace for all people.

Believe and enjoy!

PRAYER

God the Spirit, have your way in me. Shine your light on the secret sins of my heart. Equip me for tasks that are too large for me. Make me glad in what delights you. Intercede for me and open my eyes to rightly understand the Word of truth. Amen.

REFLECTION QUESTIONS

» It is impossible for you to be somewhere that the Presence of God is not. What comes to your mind as you reflect on that?
» Your body is a container for the Spirit of Jesus. What difference ought that to make in you?
» Reflect on two realities the Spirit brings to you: Comfort and Power. How do you need each one of these in your life today?
» What is the most amazing thing the Holy Spirit has done in your life?
» Practice this week's memory verse.

CONVERSATION 1 DISCUSSION
WHO IS GOD?

Truth #1 God is the Sovereign Creator
Truth #2 God is the Comprehensive Sustainer of All things
Truth #3 He is One God Existing in Three Persons
Truth #4 God is Merciful and Just
Truth #5 God is with Us

Gather with your Pursuit Group and have the following discussion:

» Take turns reciting this Week's memory verse: 2 Samuel 7:22
» How has it been helpful to reflect on that verse every day?
» Does the idea of God's Sovereignty comfort you or confront you? Why?
» What are three ways you might demonstrate complete submission to God's authority in your life?
» No matter whether you choose submission or rebellion, God already knew it in advance, and will use it for His sovereign plan. How do you feel about that?
» Where are you when you feel closest to God?
» Do you have a tendency to tell God how big your problems are, or tell your problems how big your God is? Why is that your tendency?
» If God were to speak to your current fears or anxieties right now, what would He say?
» Why do you think God chose to reveal Himself to us in three Persons?
» How is knowing God as Father helpful or difficult for you?
» What would it be like to deeply desire mercy for everyone?
» God says that if we confess our sin, He is faithful and just to forgive them. How deeply do you believe this? What is it like for someone to stake their life on this?
» It is impossible for you to be somewhere that the Presence of God is not. What comes to mind as you reflect on that?
» Your body is a container for the Spirit of Jesus. What difference ought that to make in you?
» The Holy Spirit brings comfort and power to you. How do you need each one of those in your life today?
» Make a group decision on a one-sentence answer to the question, "Who is God" and write it in your 40 Day Pursuit Guides.
» Share one way you need to experience God right now. Pray for each other.

CONVERSATION 2
WHAT IS MAN?

WEEK 2 INTRODUCTION

There are two beliefs that inform your identity more than any other: what you believe about God, and what you believe about you. These two beliefs shape almost everything about how you see and interpret life, love, meaning, value, and eternity. Regardless of how deeply you consciously think about these, all of your sense of self, purpose, and meaning stem from this quiet, or not so quiet, debate inside you. Last week we learned about who God is. This week we will explore who God says you are.

The health of a person's soul can be determined by the cohesion of three internal pillars: Identity (who and Whose I am), Faith (what and why I believe), and Character (consistently living out who I am and what I believe). The soul is at peace when these three pillars are aligned, and the soul is in conflict when they are not. Because we are made by Him and for Him, it is He who knows how to calibrate all three of these pillars. As we anchor our identity in Him, place our faith in Him, and align our behavioral compass to His true north, our soul finds its rest in Him.

WEEK 2 MEMORY VERSE

 "See what great love the Father has lavished on us, that we should be called children of God! And that is what we are!"

1 John 3:1

TRUTH #6
MAN IS AN IMAGE BEARER

QUOTE

"I am made in the image of God. Therefore, if I do not know God, I cannot know me."
- **Craig D. Lounsbrough**

SCRIPTURE

"Then God said, "Let us make mankind in our image, in our likeness, so that they may rule over the fish in the sea and the birds in the sky, over the livestock and all the wild animals, and over all the creatures that move along the ground." So God created mankind in his own image, in the image of God he created them; male and female he created them."
- **Genesis 1:26-27**

DEVOTIONAL

A common practice of all ancient religions is the worship of images; idols, statues, and figurines - each designed to represent a specific god. Upon these, people were to pay homage, worship, or sacrifice according to their religion. The God of the Bible stands alone among the ancient faiths as the only One who not only has no images made of Him, but absolutely forbids that any be made. Why? Because He has made that image with His own two hands, in the making of mankind.

Men and women were made by God to bear His image, individually and in community with one another, and to do so by ruling over His creation on His behalf. The implications of this are staggering! As image-bearers, we see that our greatest glory is to reflect His glory well. Conversely, the ugliest thing an image-bearer can do is to seek to make an image of himself, for himself and his own glory. Your life was made to glorify God and it is in glorifying Him that you experience the immense glory you were made to behold.

Being image-bearers also means that there is no human being on earth that does not reflect God. No matter how much we smear, distort, or reject His image in us, the image remains, for it is eternal. And in the most beautiful act of God's character, He, whose image we bear, makes himself into our image, to come and redeem us. Jesus comes as the "son of man" that He can join our suffering, redeem our failure, and restore us to the King who made us for Himself.

> *"He who did not spare His own Son, but gave Him up for us all - how will He not also, along with Him, graciously give us all things?"* **- Romans 8:32**

PRAYER

Maker of All, let me not lose sight that I, and every human being you have made, are created in your image. Never let me doubt this about myself. Never let me doubt this about any other man or woman, for to do so denies you the glory that is due to your name. Help me reflect you well in my world and to bring you glory today. Amen.

REFLECTION QUESTIONS

» Make a list of the ways human beings reflect the image of God.
» God made us in His image to "rule over" creation. How can we do that in a way that reflects how He rules over us?
» In what ways do you, designed to bear His image, seek instead to craft your own image for your own glory?
» Practice this week's memory verse.

_____

_____

_____

_____

_____

_____

_____

_____

TRUTH #7
MAN HAS REBELLED AGAINST GOD

QUOTE

"Whenever you see confusion, you can be sure that something is wrong. Disorder in the world implies that something is out of place. Usually, at the heart of all disorder you will find man in rebellion against God. It began in the Garden of Eden and continues to this day."
- A. W. Tozer

SCRIPTURE

"There is no one righteous, not even one; there is no one who understands; there is no one who seeks God. All have turned away, they have together become worthless; there is no one who does good, not even one."
- Romans 3:11-12

DEVOTIONAL

God created us to love, enjoy, glorify, and obey him, and by doing so, to flourish. Why then do we struggle so much to do that? Like a complicated and delicate piece of machinery that's broken we don't operate the way we were designed to, and that is because of the fall of man in the Garden of Eden.

God created humans with the capacity to keep his law perfectly, but that was lost when the first representative of the human race, Adam, seeking to be like God, chose to rebel and disobey Him. He fell into a condition of sin and dragged us all down with him. The Bible describes that condition in a variety of ways—spiritual rebellion, blindness, illness, bondage, and death.

As a result of the fall of man we are not just spiritually impaired, but completely broken. We are not just weak; we have no innate power at all to obey God's law and glorify him. We are estranged from our Creator, from one another, and from the rest of creation. In this spiritually disabled condition, we're unable to obey God's law even in our thoughts, attitudes, and motivations. "The heart is deceitful above all things, and desperately sick; who can understand it?" (Jeremiah 17:19).

Therefore, we stand alienated and guilty before the holy God of heaven and earth.

But how did Adam's sin find its way to me? Through the bloodstream. God has always forbidden the eating of blood because life is in the blood. So is sin. The life and sin of our fathers is passed on to us through the process of conception. That's a very discouraging thing to consider, of course, but it is just the beginning of the story. To rescue us, God decided to give birth to the son of man whose veins contain the blood, not of fallen man, but of God himself. This perfect blood accomplishes for us what we can never accomplish on our own - perfect atonement.

PRAYER

Merciful Lord, I am corrupt in my very nature. I am a son or daughter of the first Adam, and I constantly desire what you forbid. Give me a new nature through new birth in Christ, the second Adam, that I might be able to keep your law in the power of the Holy Spirit. Amen.

REFLECTION QUESTIONS

» Humanism says man is basically good while the Bible teaches that man is basically broken. What difference does it make where you start?
» Where do you see the consequences of rebellion in your own life?
» What kind of death have you experienced because of your sin?
» Talk to God about the pain you have experienced and the pain you have caused.
» Practice this week's memory verse.

TRUTH #8
MAN IS UTTERLY DEPRAVED

QUOTE

"The depravity of man is at once the most empirically verifiable reality but at the same time the most intellectually resisted fact."
- Malcolm Muggeridge

SCRIPTURE

"The heart is deceitful above all things and beyond cure. Who can understand it?"
- Jeremiah 17:9

DEVOTIONAL

As every parent can testify, all young children must be taught to say "please" and "thank you" and to share. But you never have to encourage a child to say "mine!" or to grab things that don't belong to them or to hoard their toys from others. Even as adults, we have to discipline ourselves to say kind and encouraging things, but it takes no discipline at all to be critical, negative, or judgmental.

Now this does not mean that people are devoid of all goodness. We are made in God's image; therefore, we all are still capable of doing good and beautiful things. But sin has corrupted our ability to love and obey God with our whole hearts, strength, and minds. Sin has infected every part of us so that we are all born in sin and guilt, corrupt in our nature, and unable to keep God's law perfectly.

Imagine there is a hungry lion, and imagine putting two plates of food in front of him—one plate of raw red meat, and the other, a plate of a perfectly prepared vegetable medley. The lion can choose either one, but because of his nature, he's always going to choose the red meat. The problem is even worse: we are not just depraved in our nature - we are dead in our trespasses and sins. But thankfully, Christ did not come to make bad people good. He came to make dead people alive.

This transformation is far more dramatic than many of us allow ourselves to believe. Jesus didn't suffer death so you could be nicer to people; He died and rose again both for your salvation, and so that you may have a new heart. A heart that desires what God desires, through the work of the Spirit and to no credit of your own. This process is so radical that the Bible refers to it many times as being born all over again.

> *"Therefore, if anyone is in Christ, he is a new creation. The old has passed away; behold, the new has come."*
> **- 2 Corinthians 5:17**

PRAYER

Holy God, left to my own devices, I transgress your law at every turn. I have no defense, but must plead guilty before your throne of judgment. Your law condemns me and cuts through my justifications and excuses, convincing me that I desperately need a Savior. Forgive my sin, Lord Jesus, and be my Savior. Amen.

REFLECTION QUESTIONS

- » People resist the idea of total depravity. Why do you think that is?
- » How much do you still naturally attempt to defend your nature as basically good and your intentions as always genuine?
- » What does it mean to be dead in your trespasses and sin?
- » What does it mean to be made alive again?
- » Practice this week's memory verse.

TRUTH #9
MAN IS THE CENTRAL OBJECT OF GOD'S AFFECTION

QUOTE

"God carries your picture in His wallet ."
- **Anthony Campolo**

SCRIPTURE

"Keep me as the apple of your eye; hide me in the shadow of your wings."
- **Psalm 17:8**

DEVOTIONAL

During the week of creation, God finished five of the days saying, "and it was good." But after the sixth day, he finished by saying, "and it was *very* good." It was indeed a great day, for that was the day God had crafted man with His own hands, after His own image, and breathed into his nostrils the breath of life. And man became a living soul; an image bearer; a ruler called to exercise dominion over the rest of creation as a reflection of God's nature; a friend of God with whom He walked in the cool of the day. You and I have never known a parent, spouse, child, grandchild, or friend whom we have loved as genuinely and purely as God loves us.

It is noteworthy that there is only one thing in all of the creation account that is considered, "not good." The Lord God said, "it is not good for the man to be alone" (Genesis 2:18). This passage refers to the fact that, for a period of time, Adam had no other person to relate to. God judged that this solitude of man was not good, even though he was surrounded by beauty, amazing animals, and direct access to God. Man needed another human being to be his companion, partner, and friend. God is not jealous *of* us, but is jealous *for* us to find all that He had in mind when He made us.

Think about this:

The same God who created the universe knows us completely. He cares for us and loves us. He delights over us with singing. He wants a relationship with us and He takes the initiative to reveal Himself to us, and to help us respond to, and offer, love. He does all of this at great personal cost to Himself. "God so loved the world that He gave..." (John 3:16). He never stops giving.

PRAYER

God my Maker, in life and in death, I cast myself on your merciful, fatherly care. You love me because I am your own. I have no good apart from you, and I could ask for no greater gift than to belong to you. Help me to know you even as I am fully known. Amen.

REFLECTION QUESTIONS

» What are the implications for your life, that the God of all Creation loves you this much?
» What does it mean that God is not jealous *of* you, but jealous *for* you?
» How do you see God's love and care in your life?
» How are you responding to God's desire to have a relationship with you? How can you grow that relationship?
» Write out a prayer expressing your thoughts about God's unstoppable and sacrificial love for you. Write of your gratitude and sorrow. Stand in awe of His works.
» Practice this week's memory verse.

TRUTH #10
MAN WAS MADE TO GLORIFY GOD

QUOTE

"We are half-hearted creatures, fooling about with drink and sex and ambition when infinite joy is offered us. We are like an ignorant child who wants to go on making mud pies in a slum because he cannot imagine what is meant by the offer of a holiday at the sea. We are far too easily pleased."
- C. S. Lewis

SCRIPTURE

"Rejoice in the Lord always; again I will say, rejoice!"
- Philippians 4:4

DEVOTIONAL

The Westminster Catechism states that, "the chief end of man is to know God and enjoy Him forever." God made us in His image, to freely share His glory with us. As image-bearers, we were made to relish in God - to delight in Him and celebrate Him "with joy inexpressible and full of glory." (1 Peter 1:8) This joy is the natural outcome of a new life in Christ, and with it also comes gratitude, praise, and glory to God.

The world rings with praise. Men praise their spouses, fans praise their favorite player, hikers praise the wilderness, singers praise their favorite song. Man was made to praise, and no matter how far he finds himself from God, it remains evident that he was designed with that in mind. Just as men praise what they value, they urge us to join along in praise as well. "Isn't she lovely?" "Wasn't that awesome?" "Isn't that guy amazing?"

When the Psalmist urges us to join along with him in praising his glorious God, he is doing what we all do. He is prompting us to praise the God who does all things well and whose nature is observed throughout creation. This is exactly how we glorify God - by declaring our great love for Him and the incredible value He has added to our lives, and by helping others to praise Him too.

You can achieve all of your earthly dreams, experience every adventure you ever imagined, and be the object of everyone's admiration, but if your life fails to glorify God, you will lack the stable foundation upon which all of life is designed to be built. Without that foundation you will feel unsafe, awkward, and vulnerable. This is a life that is lived in pursuit of the praise of man, rather than of the praise of God. Save yourself the stress, pain, and loss now; choose knowing, enjoying, and bringing glory to God as your main objective in life.

PRAYER

Heavenly Father, you have saved me from sin. Let me not continue in it as if I were still enslaved to it. I praise you for I am fearfully and wonderfully made. Help me to praise and glorify you above all things. May all who know me see my good works and glorify you because of them. Amen.

REFLECTION QUESTIONS

- » Referring to the C. S. Lewis quote above, in what ways are you too easily pleased, rather than reaching for more?
- » Finish this sentence: Lord, I rejoice in you today because...
- » Have you had times where success, money, or popularity failed to deliver what you thought they might? What is that hole these things cannot fill?
- » Today, every time you touch your keys or stick your hand into your pocket, let it be a trigger to praise God for how good He is. Do that all day today.
- » Practice the memory verse.

CONVERSATION 2 DISCUSSION
WHAT IS MAN?

Truth #6   Man is an Image Bearer
Truth #7   Man has Rebelled Against God
Truth #8   Man is Utterly Depraved
Truth #9   Man is the Central Object of God's Affection
Truth #10 Man was Made to Glorify God

Gather with your Pursuit Group and have the following discussion:

» Take turns reciting this Week's memory verse: 1 John 3:1
» What are some ways human beings reflect the image of God?
» In what ways do you, designed to bear the image of God, seek instead to craft your own image for your own glory?
» Humanism says that man is basically good while the Bible teaches that man is fundamentally broken. What difference does it make where you start?
» What does it mean that man is utterly depraved? Why is it important to know this?
» Where do you see the consequences of rebellion in your own life?
» Many people resist the idea of total depravity. Why do you think that is?
» What does it mean to be dead in your trespasses and sin?
» What does it mean to be made alive again?
» How do you see God's love and care in your life?
» How can you grow in your relationship with God?
» What from this week, if anything, is a bit confusing to you? What questions do you have?
» Make a group decision on a one-sentence answer to the question, "What is Man?" and write it in your 40 Day Pursuit Guides.
» Two weeks in, how is The Pursuit going for you?
» Share prayer requests and current life issues with one another.
» Pray for each other.

CONVERSATION 3
WHAT DOES GOD REQUIRE OF US?

WEEK 3 INTRODUCTION

Religion is man's attempt to understand, satisfy, and win the favor of God. And the world has always been full of all kinds of religions, as people try to find the secret to pleasing the gods. This desire to understand God is hard-wired into the heart of man, for the human soul retains in its DNA the memory of the Garden of Eden and instinctively seeks to find its way home. But how does God desire to be pursued and known?

WEEK 3 MEMORY VERSE

"Love the Lord your God with all your heart and with all your soul and with all your mind and with all your strength.' The second is this: 'Love your neighbor as yourself.' There is no commandment greater than these."

Mark 12:30-31

TRUTH #11
GOD'S LAW IS STATED IN THE TEN COMMANDMENTS

QUOTE

"Because God created and loves us and knows what's best for us, he gives us moral and spiritual direction about how to live life in the best way. The Ten Commandments are a love gift to us from God. Of course this is true of all Scripture, but the heart and soul of God's guidance is found in the Ten Commandments."
- John Yates

SCRIPTURE

"You shall have no other gods before me."
- Exodus 20:3

DEVOTIONAL

Man first encountered God in the Garden of Eden, where he had direct access to Him and often walked with Him in the cool of the day. It was an amazing world - beauty, animals, no rain, no sin, no pain or sickness - and it was all he knew. Then, because of his suspicion that God might be holding out on him, he chose to eat the fruit of the tree of the Knowledge of Good and Evil (It is commonly called an apple, but I prefer to think of it as a mango because I really like apples).

And then all hell broke loose.

After being cursed for his rebellion, exiled from the Garden and separated from God's Presence, man found himself living in a broken world where now all things go from order to chaos, and from life to death. He longed for God and God longed for him, so God made a way for man to reconnect with Him. This way to reconnect is the Law. It is justice and mercy, as man deals directly with his sin and leans into obedience to God for His grace, blessing, and favor.

The Ten Commandments were given by God as the perfect Law that defines what God wants from us. They guide us to living the life

He had in mind when He made us. They are the first answer to the question, "What does God require of us?"

Wherever any person, family, community, or nation follows these laws, justice rules, relationships flourish, and God's favor is found in abundance. So much is this true that the Ten Commandments once hung in every courthouse of our country, acknowledging that they provide the foundation for our laws and legal system. These commandments speak universally to every culture and reveal the heart issues of every person. The result is that they reveal the holiness of God and the depravity of man, setting the table for the coming of a Savior to rescue us from the Law by satisfying its demands for us.

PRAYER

Holy God, you have continued to reveal your love to your people by giving us your commandments, that we may find favor with you. May I always give thanks for your law. You have not left me ignorant of how to walk in the way of righteousness with you. Help me to glorify your Name by obeying your Ten Commandments by the grace of Jesus and through the power of your Holy Spirit. Amen.

REFLECTION QUESTIONS

» Describe what it means, in a single sentence, to have no other gods before Him in your life.
» How are the Ten Commandments a gift from God to us?
» Like Adam and Eve, do you ever wonder if God is withholding something from you? If so, why?
» Practice the memory verse.

CONVERSATION 3 **WHAT DOES GOD REQUIRE OF US?**

TRUTH #12
NOBODY CAN KEEP GOD'S LAW PERFECTLY

QUOTE

"As a result of the fall we're not just spiritually impaired but incapacitated. We're not just weak; we have no innate power to obey God's law and glorify him. We're estranged from our Creator, from one another, and from the rest of creation."
- **Leo Schuster**

SCRIPTURE

"None is righteous, no, not one; no one understands; no one seeks for God. All have turned aside; together they have become worthless; no one does good, not even one."
- **Romans 3:10-12**

DEVOTIONAL

In Romans 3, God makes His assessment of mankind painfully clear: all of us have turned away from Him and have become worthless; none of us does good or seeks for God. The great human rebellion against God has resulted in a tragic reality: all are now born with hearts that are deceitful and beyond cure. We don't even recognize or understand the complexities of our own hearts. (Jeremiah 17:9) We are fundamentally broken, and we lack the insight to fully grasp how broken we are.

This is horrible news, yet it is important to recognize that it's not the *end* of the story, but the beginning. It is the bad news that sets the table for the good news of Jesus Christ, who kept God's Law perfectly and offered Himself as a substitute for us. All who trust in Him are justified through faith and restored to God. They are set free from bondage, guilt, and shame. This is a gift from God, through faith, by the power of His Spirit in us.

"For just as through the disobedience of the one man the many were made sinners, so also through the obedience of the one man the many will be made righteous." (Romans 5:19) We all fell with Adam, but we have been raised with Christ. The God who raised Jesus from the dead is powerfully at work in us and won't let us go. Remind yourself of this often. Even though Christ is alive in us, our sinful nature also remains very much engaged.

Even after we have met Jesus, we cannot obey God's law perfectly. Our flesh just won't roll over and quit, so the battle of sin rages on. We can, however, practice victory daily as we walk by the Spirit and not by the flesh. This is accomplished moment-by-moment as we quiet our flesh and actively surrender to the desires and power of the Spirit of Christ in us.

One day He will bring us into His everlasting Presence, where we will no longer battle our flesh. There we will finally, freely, fully, and forever obey the One who made us His own.

PRAYER

Holy God, I was born already broken and have transgressed your law at every turn. I have lived for myself and not for you. Even my best efforts at loving you fall short of true purity and love. Thank you for forgiving me and restoring me through Jesus Christ, my Lord. Help me to live in Him and through Him, by the Presence and power of your grace upon me. Amen.

REFLECTION QUESTIONS

» Do you believe that man is born good and turns bad through the contamination of this world OR that man is born already broken and incapable of true goodness? What difference does it make?
» Do you truly believe that life works best only when it is lived in God, for God, and in obedience to God? Is there an arena of your life where you fail to practice this belief?
» When life is lived in and for God, He becomes the source of our Identity. Where do you find your identity? (God? Money? Popularity? Success? Other?)
» Practice the memory verse.

TRUTH #13
THE PURPOSE OF THE LAW IS TO SHOW US OUR SIN

QUOTE

"The law bids us, as we try to fulfill its requirements, and become wearied in our weakness under it, to know how to ask for the help of grace."
- **St. Augustine**

SCRIPTURE

"I found that the very commandment that was intended to bring life actually brought death. For sin, seizing the opportunity afforded by the commandment, deceived me, and through the commandment put me to death."
- **Romans 7:10-11**

DEVOTIONAL

God forbid Adam to eat of the forbidden tree, not as a barrier to self-actualization, but as a gracious gift. The fruit of that tree was not a path to goodness, but a path to death, and God wanted to protect him from it. The Ten Commandments are, likewise, a gift, designed to show us how to live joyful lives of abundance while avoiding loss, pain, and death. The Law is righteous and good, however, because of my depravity, I am incapable of living a law-abiding life. The Law holds up a mirror so that I might see the ugliness of my inner, rebellious self and turn my heart toward the God whose grace alone can make me whole.

In Romans 7, Paul says, "I would not have known what coveting really was if the Law had not said, 'You shall not covet.'" (v7). But knowing the law, and grasping what the law asks of me does not help me defeat my sin - it just reveals to me what I really am: a broken and desperate sinner. We need more than rules to set us free. The law is only God's first gift to us; the second is His fulfillment of that same law on our behalf, and in our stead.

Of course, the Law does other things too. Obedience to the Law distinguishes the people of God from all other people on the earth, and it guides us into the righteous life God designed for us. But first the Law breaks us, shows us the endless depth of our depravity, and forces us to confront our desperate need of a Savior. God's hope is that the ugly brutality of my brokenness will drive me to my knees in repentant dependence upon Jesus, and His redemptive work in me. There are only two kinds of people in the world: sinners who admit it and sinners who don't.

PRAYER

Holy Father, thank you for the Law that kills me so that the Spirit can give me life. I confess my inability to keep your Law and my slavery to sin. Thank you for being the one who frees the captives and bears my burdens. I look to you for my strength today. Amen.

REFLECTION QUESTIONS

- » Walk through the Ten Commandments (Exodus 20) and count the ones you have broken.
- » How do rules awaken my rebellious nature? Why is that true of both kids and adults?
- » Think of the last commandment you broke. Why did you break it? What were you hoping to gain? If you have not confessed to God, do it now.
- » Practice the memory verse.

TRUTH #14
SIN IS LAWLESSNESS

QUOTE

"Sin is a fundamental relationship; it is not wrong doing, it is wrong being, deliberate and empathic independence of God."
- Oswald Chambers

SCRIPTURE

"Everyone who makes a practice of sinning also practices lawlessness; sin is lawlessness."
- 1 John 3:4

DEVOTIONAL

All sinful behaviors and choices are the same sin, and that sin is rebellion against God: rejection of his rule over our lives. Sin is living without reference to God, not viewing him as the defining authority of our lives, around which our entire being needs to be centered. It is believing that you know better than He, and then acting on that belief.

Consider our solar system: It is perfectly designed and it works as intended because it operates within that design. The slightest degree of variation of Earth's rotation or orbit, for example, would render our planet uninhabitable. What would happen if some of the planets decided not to orbit the sun? Or to create their own orbits, around whatever object they desired? Or refused to orbit at all? The answer is death and destruction. The solar system as we know it would unravel and fall apart because the planets would not be orbiting the correct center. They would not be living in reference to the sun, and everything would fall apart and be destroyed.

Life works best when lived in full surrender and obedience to the laws and ways of God. It was designed carefully by God that way, for our guidance, favor, and blessing. God invites us to leverage His ways for our own good, but our stubborn hearts and self-centered egos are not convinced. We trust our three pounds of brain to outsmart God and His design.

The reality is that the wisest person on earth; the most shrewd thinker; the most selfish decision-maker ever, would choose obedience to God as their path because they would understand that it is absolutely the best path for them. But our sin-nature doesn't allow for this, and we rebel. We choose lawlessness. We choose sin.

PRAYER

Lord of the Universe, all your ways are good. I pursue the way of death and destruction when I go my own way. Help me to see sin as the lie and poison that it truly is. Help me to allow your law, rather than my spirit of lawlessness, to shape my mind and my life. Amen.

REFLECTION QUESTIONS

» When was the last time you chose to trust your own thinking and plans rather than God's clear direction for your life? How did that work out for you?

» On a scale of 0-10, how much do you actually believe that obedience and submission to God and His ways is absolutely the most rewarding and safe thing a person can do? (remember that if your answer truly is 10, you'd never rebel)

» Focus today on confident trust - that if you obey God, it will serve you well.

» Practice the memory verse.

TRUTH #15
JESUS SATISFIES THE LAW OF GOD

QUOTE

"Begotten by the Father, He was not made by the Father; He was made Man in the Mother whom He Himself had made, so that He might exist here for a while, sprung from her who could never and nowhere have existed except through His power."
- **Augustine of Hippo**

SCRIPTURE

"Do not think that I have come to abolish the Law or the Prophets; I have not come to abolish them but to fulfill them. For truly I tell you, until heaven and earth disappear, not the smallest letter, not the least stroke of a pen, will by any means disappear from the Law until everything is accomplished."
- **Jesus (Matthew 5:17-18)**

DEVOTIONAL

God is Holy and Just, and while obedience to His Law is required and rewarded, disobedience must be punished. God told Adam that if he ate the fruit of the forbidden tree then he would surely die. So, when this command was broken, death entered into the human experience and we were banished from the Garden. Now life *and* death flow in the veins of human beings.

Because life is in the blood, God has always forbidden the eating of the blood of animals and required accountability for the shedding of human blood. He also established that without death (the shedding of blood), sin cannot be forgiven. In fact, the law requires that without the shedding of blood there is no forgiveness. (Hebrews 9:22)

We have all broken God's Law and there is no forgiveness for this rebellion without the shedding of blood - the giving of a life.

Enter Jesus, who is born of a virgin (the sin-infected blood of a human father is not in Him) and lived His life in perfect obedience to God the Father. He obeyed the Laws of God perfectly. Because of His great love for us, "God made him who had no sin to be sin for us, so that in him we might become the righteousness of God." (2 Corinthians 5:21) The blood of life was shed to defeat the death that flows in our veins. His perfect obedience is credited to us and satisfies our sin-debt. His death is the ultimate fulfillment of the law, while simultaneously the most merciful gift God has ever given. Justice is served and Holiness remains in tact, for disobedience is punished and obedience is rewarded - all in the person of Jesus.

PRAYER

Precious Redeemer, before the world began, you loved me. You gave up your glory to bear my shame. You glorified the Father by obeying Him all the way to the cross. You deserve my praise, my gratitude, and my worship. I have no hope but in you, so in you I place all of my hope. Amen.

REFLECTION QUESTIONS

» If you die today and God asks you why He should allow you into His heaven, what will you say? (hint: there is only one Biblically correct answer)
» If Jesus' blood gives you eternal life, how does that affect how you see yourself in this life?
» There is not one thing in all of creation more powerful than the shed blood of Jesus. Meditate on this for a minute and give thanks to God.
» Practice the memory verse.

CONVERSATION 3 DISCUSSION WHAT DOES GOD REQUIRE OF US?

Truth #11 God's Law is Stated in the 10 Commandments
Truth #12 Nobody Can Keep God's Law Perfectly
Truth #13 The Purpose of the Law is to Show Us Our Sin
Truth #14 Sin is Lawlessness
Truth #15 Jesus Satisfies the Law of God

Gather with your Pursuit Group and have the following discussion:

» Take turns reciting this Week's memory verse: Mark 12:30-31
» What does God require of us?
» Do you ever feel like God is holding out on you? Explain.
» In what ways are you too easily pleased, instead of reaching for more?
» Where do you find your personal sense of identity?
» On a scale of 1-10, how convinced are you that full submission to God is the best plan for your success?
» In what arena of life do you fail to practice God's plan for you?
» How are the 10 Commandments a gift from God to us?
» How do rules awaken our rebellious nature? Why is this true?
» If Jesus can be trusted with our eternal sin-problem, why do we struggle to trust Him for our daily problems?
» What does it mean to love God with all you've got?
» Have you had times where success, or money, or hitting a goal failed to deliver what you thought they might? What is the hole these things cannot fill?
» How is the Pursuit going for you so far?
» Share prayer requests and current life issues with one another.
» Pray for each other.

CONVERSATION 4
WHO IS JESUS?

WEEK 4 INTRODUCTION

Jesus is the most pivotal, controversial, and influential person in history! The marking of time is defined by His life, His teachings are considered the most beautiful ideals ever expressed, and billions of people claim to have had their lives changed by Him. He was raised by a carpenter, lived in a rural and politically powerless region of the world, and never traveled more than 200 miles from home. He claimed to be the Son of God and it got Him executed. He predicted his execution and promised his resurrection. Truly He is the most interesting man in the world.

WEEK 4 MEMORY VERSE

≈ *"Therefore, since we have a great high priest who has ascended into heaven, Jesus the Son of God, let us hold firmly to the faith we profess."*

Hebrews 4:14

TRUTH #16
JESUS IS THE HERO OF ALL CREATION

QUOTE

"Jesus of Nazareth, without money and arms, conquered more millions than Alexander the Great, Caesar, Mohammed, and Napoleon; without science and learning, he shed more light on things human and divine than all philosophers and scholars combined; without the eloquence of school, he spoke such words of life as were never spoken before or since; without writing a single line, he set more pens in motion, and furnished themes for more sermons, orations, discussions, learned volumes, works of art, and songs of praise than the whole army of great men of ancient and modern times."
- Philip Schaff

SCRIPTURE

"Through him all things were made; without him nothing was made that has been made. In him was life, and that life was the light of all mankind. The light shines in the darkness, and the darkness has not overcome it."
- John 1:3

DEVOTIONAL

The history of the world is His story; the story of God. We were made by Him, for Him, and through Him. And the crown jewel, the pinnacle, the climax of the story and the Hero that changes everything is Jesus. Jesus is the author of the story, the purpose of the story, the beginning, and the end of the story. And the hero of every great story written by man follows the model of this Hero.

"The Hero's Journey" is a concept popularized in "The Hero with a Thousand Faces" by Joseph Campbell. Campbell says the hero of every story shares a common journey and it goes like this: the hero receives a call to action and leaves his home for a strange land, where there are mysterious and supernatural forces. The hero faces trials and victories, but eventually finds himself in "the abyss" or "the cave," where he is at his lowest and most hopeless point. The hero then overcomes the abyss, achieves his final and greatest triumph, and returns home with a power or prize he won on his journey. You may recognize this pattern in some of your favorite stories, and it is at its purest in the story of our ultimate Hero and Savior, Jesus.

Jesus, who was in eternity with His Father, left glory and honor to dwell in human form on earth. He did this for the redemption and reconciliation of mankind; this was His call to action. In His mission on earth, Jesus did many wonders and had victories over enemies, but eventually made His way to the abyss - where Jesus, crying out to His Father in pain, died on the cross. Yet, just as the heroes of myth overcome, Jesus overcame death itself and not only walked out of the grave, but walked out with the keys of death and hell in His hands.

With His great victory, Jesus returned home to reunite with His Father. And the prize He returned with, the hero's gift in our earthly stories, was the ultimate defeat of death and damnation. This victory is ours in Him, and is our only hope in life and in death.

PRAYER

Jesus, I join with all of creation and celebrate you, THE Hero. Thank you for laying aside your glory, joining in my battle, defeating my enemy once and for all, and giving me your Spirit as my prize and future. You are my victory and all of my hope is in you. Amen.

REFLECTION QUESTIONS

> » We will enjoy the victory of Jesus in its fullness one day. What victory can we enjoy today?
> » Hold your keys in your hand. All day, every time you touch your keys, remind yourself that your Hero, Jesus, has conquered your enemy completely.
> » The Holy Spirit is the key to knowing and living the victory of Jesus every day. Ask the Holy Spirit to heighten your awareness of His Presence and Help with you today.
> » Practice the memory verse.

TRUTH #17
JESUS IS THE EXACT REPRESENTATION OF GOD'S NATURE

QUOTE

"If you have seen me, you have seen the Father."
- Jesus Christ

SCRIPTURE

"In the past God spoke to our ancestors through the prophets at many times and in various ways, but in these last days he has spoken to us by his Son, whom he appointed heir of all things, and through whom also he made the universe. The Son is the radiance of God's glory and the exact representation of his being..."
- Hebrews 1:2-3

DEVOTIONAL

If we want to know what God is like, we need only to look at Jesus. Everything we read and understand about God through the Bible is most accurately read through the lens of Jesus. He is the ultimate revelation of God.

The key to understanding the Bible is Jesus. The key to understanding God's character is Jesus. The key to getting our lives sorted out is Jesus. We do not need Jesus-and-angels. We do not need Jesus-and-Moses. We do not need Jesus-and-Mary. We do not need Jesus-and-a-priest. All we need is Jesus.

This is enormously helpful when we struggle to imagine how God feels about us, or how God might respond to our failures, or how God feels about this broken, sick, and depraved world of ours. When we seek to understand how God responds to messed up, fallen, and helpless people, we only need to watch how Jesus responds to them. The heart of Jesus toward the "least of these" is the exact representation of God's heart toward me. And that heart always pursues redemption, restoration, and reconciliation.

The God of the Old Testament says, "Do I take any pleasure in the death of the wicked? declares the Sovereign Lord. Rather, am I not pleased when they turn from their ways and live?" (Ezekiel 18:23) Likewise, Jesus said "there will be more rejoicing in heaven over one sinner who repents than over ninety-nine righteous persons who do not need to repent." (Luke 15:7)

How will you find God? By looking at Jesus Christ, because He alone was God in human flesh. You don't have to rely exclusively on your search for God because He has already searched for you!

PRAYER

Lord, thank you that, because of Jesus, your presence is no longer covered with a cloud. I can see you more clearly and talk to you more intimately. Thank you that I can lift up my heart and hands to you. You restore me to yourself and you renew me. Thank you for Jesus. Thank you that the key to life is in Jesus. Thank you that I can know and understand who you are through Jesus. Amen.

REFLECTION QUESTIONS

- » Jesus helps us see the Father. What confusions do you have about the Father that Jesus might resolve?
- » Jesus is in the Father and you are in Jesus. What does this mean to you?
- » If you could ask Jesus one question today, what would it be? (Go ahead and ask Him)
- » Practice the memory verse.

TRUTH #18
JESUS IS THE MEDIATOR
BETWEEN GOD AND MAN

QUOTE

"He (God) is not a mere mortal like me that I might answer him, that we might confront each other in court. If only there were someone to mediate between us, someone to bring us together, someone to remove God's rod from me, so that his terror would frighten me no more."
- Job

SCRIPTURE

" For there is one God and one mediator between God and mankind, the man Christ Jesus, who gave himself as a ransom for all people."
- 1 Timothy 2:5-6

DEVOTIONAL

A mediator is someone who helps two parties reach an agreement, especially when they are at odds; one who acts as an intermediary to work with opposing sides in order to bring about a settlement. Another word for that is an advocate - one who speaks in favor of, or argues on behalf of, another. Ever since man sinned and rebelled against God, we have been separated from Him, for God had a dispute with us because of sin.

Sin is described in the Bible as transgression of the law of God and rebellion against God. God hates sin, and sin stands between all of us and Him. "There is no one righteous, not even one." (Romans 3:10) All human beings are sinners by virtue of both the sin we have inherited from Adam, as well as the sin we commit on a daily basis. The only just penalty for this sin is death (Romans 6:23): not only physical death, but eternal death.

Nothing we could do on our own would be sufficient to mediate between ourselves and God. No amount of good works or law-keeping makes us righteous enough to stand before a holy God (Isaiah 64:6; Romans 3:20; Galatians 2:16). Without a mediator, we are destined to spend eternity apart from God, for by ourselves, salvation from our sin is impossible.

Yet there is hope!

Jesus officially represents those who have placed their trust in Him before God's throne of judgment. He mediates for us, much like a defense attorney mediates for his client, telling the judge, "Your honor, my client is innocent of all charges against him." But in our case, the defense attorney confesses that we are guilty as charged. Rather than arguing our innocence, He instead asks to receive the punishment on our behalf. Someday we will face God, but we will do so as totally forgiven sinners because of Jesus' death for us. Verdict delivered. Sentence served. Penalty over. Forever.

PRAYER

God the Son, my mediator and advocate. Because of my sin, I deserve, but could never bear, the wrath of God and eternal death. Only you, the Holy One, could suffer the just punishment for sin and permanently defeat death. Thank you for making a path from me to God, to be able to enjoy him and you forever. Amen.

REFLECTION QUESTIONS

» Jesus now sits at the right hand of the Father, continuing to advocate for us through prayer. (Romans 8:34) How might Jesus be praying for you today?
» Jesus asks us to join in His suffering - the just suffering for the unjust, or the mature suffering for the immature. What is one way you could do that this week?
» Close your eyes and hear the judge's gavel slam with the announcement of your guilt. Then hear Jesus offer to take your punishment for you. Give thanks.
» Practice the memory verse.

TRUTH #19
JESUS IS GOD, REDEEMING MAN BACK TO HIMSELF

QUOTE

"To be supremely loving, God must give us Himself."
- John Piper

SCRIPTURE

"For God was pleased to have all His fullness dwell in Him, and through Him to reconcile to Himself all things, whether things on earth or things in heaven, by making peace through the blood of His cross."
- Colossians 1:20

DEVOTIONAL

God made us for Himself, for His own glory. He who has all power, beauty, love, and authority, had been demonstrating these among the host of heavenly beings. He decided to exercise them again and to make man in His own image, in His own likeness, for Himself. For His own glory.

And man, as one-third of the heavenly beings had already done, chose to trust his own finite wisdom and rebel against the God of eternal glory. God's response to man's rebellion is a powerful, beautiful, loving, and authoritative one - it is a response that, again, demonstrates His glory.

He who existed as the Son of God before all ages, without a beginning, decided to become the Son of Man in our time. He submitted Himself to terrible evils for our sake, though He had done no evil. He did this even though we, who were the recipients of so much good at His hands, had done nothing to deserve it. Why did He do this? For His own glory.

Jesus, the perfect and pre-existing One, lived a perfect human life to become the perfect sacrifice for sin, to redeem us perfectly to Himself. He defeated death, rebellion, and the grave and became the firstborn among many brothers and sisters, who also in Him, participate in His victory. Why did He do this? For His own glory.

One day, He will wrap up human history with a beautifully powerful and resounding victory over all evil. He will do so with perfection and finality. Why? For His own glory.

And then we, who participate in Him, will join with all creation to celebrate His power, beauty, love, and authority. We will join "every creature in heaven and on earth and under the earth and on the sea, and all that is in them, saying: "To him who sits on the throne and to the Lamb be praise and honor and glory and power, for ever and ever!" (Revelation 5:13) Why? For His own glory.

PRAYER

God of eternal power, beauty, love and authority - God of all glory, I praise You. Thank you for making me, chasing me, redeeming me, and securing me forever, for your glory. Help me today to join with all creation, in heaven and on earth, in giving you glory. Help me to behold your glory and to proclaim your beauty, because for this I was made. You are the God of glory and I worship You. Amen.

REFLECTION QUESTIONS

» Why did God make mankind in the first place? Why do we exist?
» Why is it not a selfish thing, that God made us and redeemed us for His own glory?
» Every created being will give God glory one day - together. How can you give Him glory today?
» Practice the memory verse.

TRUTH #20
JESUS WAS FULLY HUMAN

QUOTE

"What we see in Jesus is true humanity. What we see in his incarnation, his earthly life and ministry, is what humanity was meant to be, what Adam was created to be but ruined in his sin and his fall."
- Thabiti Anyabwile

SCRIPTURE

"Who, being in very nature God, did not consider equality with God something to be used to his own advantage; rather, he made himself nothing by taking the very nature of a servant, being made in human likeness."
- Philippians 2:6-7

DEVOTIONAL

We say, "to err is human," but we are wrong. Sin, selfishness, hate, jealousy, and every vile thing we know in our world is not what it is to be human; they are what it is to be a broken human. And broken humans are the only kind we know.

Until Jesus comes along.

The eternal and perfect Word, seeing that in no other way could our corruption be undone - and because, being immortal, it was impossible for Him to suffer death - takes for Himself a human body capable of death. He fills that body with Himself, making it worthy to die in the place of all. And, because of He who dwells in it, it remains incorruptible. That way, and forever, corruption can be pushed away from all by the sacrifice and resurrection of the Son of Man.

Immortal God takes on mortal flesh to be our perfect and only High Priest. The truest human; a second Adam.

"Since the children have flesh and blood, he too shared in their humanity so that by his death he might break the power of him who holds the power of death—that is, the devil— and free those who all their lives were held in slavery by their fear of death. For this reason he had to be made

like them, fully human in every way, in order that he might become a merciful and faithful high priest in service to God, and that he might make atonement for the sins of the people. Because he himself suffered when he was tempted, he is able to help those who are being tempted."
- Hebrews 2:14-15; 17-18)

"Therefore, since we have a great high priest who has ascended into heaven, Jesus the Son of God, let us hold firmly to the faith we profess. For we do not have a high priest who is unable to empathize with our weaknesses, but we have one who has been tempted in every way, just as we are—yet he did not sin. Let us then approach God's throne of grace with confidence, so that we may receive mercy and find grace to help us in our time of need." **- Hebrews 4:14-16**

PRAYER

Almighty God, Father, Son, and Spirit, I want to give you thanks. You, the immortal and perfect One, took on a body like mine and entered my world. You made yourself human and made yourself nothing, so that I could be forgiven and free. Help me use my freedom to follow your lead - to make myself nothing so that you may receive glory. I boldly enter your Presence, only because you desire it and made a way for it to happen. Fill me with your Presence today, I pray. Amen.

REFLECTION QUESTIONS

- » Jesus experienced every single temptation that you experience. How does this encourage and help you?
- » Because of Jesus, you can approach God's throne of grace with confidence, to receive mercy and find grace to help you in your time of need. Do that, boldly, for a few minutes right now.
- » Make these confessions: 1) Jesus knows my human struggles. 2) Jesus overcame my human struggles. 3) I can overcome my struggles today in Jesus.
- » Practice the memory verse.

CONVERSATION 4 DISCUSSION
WHO IS JESUS?

Truth #16 Jesus is the Hero of All Creation
Truth #17 Jesus is the Exact Representation of God's Nature
Truth #18 Jesus is the Mediator between God and Man
Truth #19 Jesus is God, Redeeming Man Back to Himself
Truth #20 Jesus was Fully Human

Gather with your Pursuit Group and have the following discussion:

» Take turns reciting this Week's memory verse: John 1:3
» You can ask Jesus any one question, and He will answer. What do you ask?
» How much of Jesus' victory can we enjoy today? Explain.
» How does the Holy Spirit help us live out daily what Jesus won for us?
» How does seeing Jesus help you understand God better?
» What about God still confuses you?
» Jesus is praying for you today. What do you think He might be praying over you right now?
» Everything exists for the glory of God. What comes to your mind after reading that? Why is this important to understand?
» We are to join Jesus in His suffering - the just for the unjust. What is one way you could do that?
» Why did God make mankind in the first place? Why do we exist?
» If God made us to glorify Himself, why is this not a selfish thing on His part?
» Jesus experienced every temptation you face. Do you believe this? How is it helpful to you?
» How can your life bring glory to God this week? Be specific.
» Because of Jesus, we can approach God's throne with confidence. Do you? Why or why not?
» How is the Pursuit going for you so far?
» Share prayer requests and current life issues with one another.
» Pray for each other.

CONVERSATION 5
WHAT IS THE GOSPEL?

WEEK 5 INTRODUCTION

The word, "Gospel" means "good news" and the news of Jesus is incredibly good! However, many of us struggle to grasp and trust the good news of God's forgiveness through Jesus for ourselves. Many of us also struggle to allow that good news to change how we see others and their failures. The gospel of Jesus Christ changes everything. When we accurately understand it, and live life in its powerful freedom, we are changed and become agents of change in the world.

WEEK 5 MEMORY VERSE

"He has saved us and called us to a holy life—not because of anything we have done but because of his own purpose and grace. This grace was given us in Christ Jesus before the beginning of time."

2 Timothy 1:9

TRUTH #21
ALL OF OUR SINS CAN BE FORGIVEN

QUOTE

"The voice of sin is loud, but the voice of forgiveness is louder."
- **Dwight L. Moody**

SCRIPTURE

"For they shall all know me, from the least of them to the greatest, declares the Lord. For I will forgive their iniquity, and I will remember their sin no more."
- **Jeremiah 31:34**

DEVOTIONAL

The Bible uses three words to define the brokenness and depravity of man. There is the word, "sin," which is an archery term for "missing the mark." This describes the reality that, no matter how hard we try, we fail to be perfect. A man may love his wife, but he does not love her perfectly. His love for her is thrown off course by his dominating love of himself.

The second word used in the Scriptures is "transgression," which describes a willful violation of the Law. A driver transgresses the law when he drives his car 80 miles per hour on a road with a 70 miles per hour speed limit. Whether we look at the Law of the 10 Commandments, or Jesus' reduction of the Law to the two commands to 1) love the Lord your God with everything you've got and 2) love all people the way you love yourself, we find that we are habitual transgressors of God's Law.

The third term God uses is "iniquity," which means "perversity," or "bentness." Iniquity describes the perversion or depravity that exists in our souls, which flows in the blood of our veins because of the sin of our fathers. Depravity, or iniquity, is in us. We are born bent. All of our sin and transgression flows from who we are - so depraved that we cannot even fully grasp the depth of our depravity. We join Paul in his declaration, "Wretched man that I am! Who can save me from this body of sin and death? Thanks be to God who delivers me through Jesus Christ our Lord!" (Romans 7:24-25)

God promises, "For I will forgive their *iniquity* and remember their sin no more," hundreds of years before the birth of Jesus. God declares not only His decision to forgive my failures, but also His decision to forgive my core self: a bent, perverted failure. Because of Jesus, your core nature of sin is forgiven and your sins are remembered no more. Your acts of sin are wiped away and your whole self is forgiven and adopted into God's family forever. He chose us to be redeemed in Him before the creation of the world! (Ephesians 1:4)

PRAYER

Holy God, I confess that it is very difficult for me to grasp your grace. There are so many terrible things I have done that flow from the ugliness of who I am. I struggle to grasp that you forgive my iniquity and remember my sins no more. Please forgive my doubts, and help me to believe. And in believing, help me to live in the joy of your great love and forgiveness today, for living free and alive gives you the glory you deserve. Amen.

REFLECTION QUESTIONS

» What is harder: accepting that God forgives you or being able to forgive yourself? Why?
» If God forgives you, but you won't forgive yourself, who has more power, God or you?
» How does being completely forgiven affect your ongoing battle with sin?
» Practice the memory verse.

TRUTH #22
JESUS RECONCILES ALL THINGS

QUOTE

"Through God's gracious efforts, a people and indeed a whole creation are freed. They are now in the kingdom of the Son, a place of complete redemption and total renewal."
- **Vermon Pierre**

SCRIPTURE

"For God was pleased to have all his fullness dwell in him, and through him to reconcile to himself all things, whether things on earth or things in heaven, by making peace through his blood, shed on the cross."
- **Colossians 1:19-20**

DEVOTIONAL

Creation is broken and needs to be reconciled to God. Physical creation, the spirit world, governments and power structures, indeed all of creation, have been broken and now move from order to chaos as they exist apart from God.

Jesus is the supreme ruler over all creation. "For in him all things were created: things in heaven and on earth, visible and invisible, whether thrones or powers or rulers or authorities; all things have been created through him and for him. He is before all things, and in him all things hold together." (Colossians 1:16-17) Because of Jesus, creation itself will one day be liberated from its slavery and decay and brought into the freedom and glory of the Son of God.

This does two things for us:

1. It gives us hope for our eternal future. All around us we see evidence of the fall in things like unjust social systems, moral cultural decline, and terrible suffering. The gospel tells us not to despair, but to have a sure and certain hope that all such things will be wiped away and permanently replaced with peace, harmony, and the healing of the nations.

2. It gives us motivation for our place in the present. Creation has not been abandoned by God. Instead, through Jesus, it has been

reclaimed by Him and will eventually be made brand new. It will one day be characterized by righteousness and beauty, rightly related to God.

We, the Church, are a prophetic expression of this new creation, and we model it for the world. We are not passive bystanders in this mess, biding our time until our Rescuer arrives. Instead, we are a community of people commissioned by God. Our faithful efforts in the world matter, as we proclaim and practice the power of the gospel to redeem and renew.

PRAYER

Jesus, the creator and redeemer of all creation, thank you that you reconcile all things and will ultimately make everything new. This gives me joy and hope. Fill me with your Spirit today, that I might model your power and grace in this world now. Amen.

REFLECTION QUESTIONS

» All things were made by Him, through Him, and for Him. Spend this day noticing how power is used, how relationships are navigated, and how money is spent. How would that be different if it was exercised by Him, through Him, and for Him?
» How can you use power, time, and money today in ways that model the redeeming and renewing work of Jesus?
» Pick one goal today, about power, humility, love, or money. How can you model that today?
» Practice the memory verse.

TRUTH #23
THE GRACE OF JESUS IS OFFERED TO ALL PEOPLE

QUOTE

"God proved His love on the Cross. When Christ hung, and bled, and died, it was God saying to the world, 'I love you.'"
- **Billy Graham**

SCRIPTURE

"For Christ's love compels us, because we are convinced that one died for all."
- **2 Corinthians 5:14**

DEVOTIONAL

God so loved the entire world that He gave His one and only Son, that whoever would believe in Him would not perish, but have everlasting life. Christ came into the world to save sinners. It is not His will that any should perish. He wants all people to be saved and to come to knowledge of the truth. Christ gave Himself as a ransom for all people. He is reconciling the world to Himself through Christ, not counting people's sins against them. He has given to us the ministry of reconciliation, as His ambassadors. So we implore you, on Christ's behalf, be reconciled to God!

That paragraph is a summation of just a few of the legion of verses in the Bible that declare God's great love for all people. Yet, in spite of this clarity, we have two common questions. The first is, "Does God really mean ME?" Can it really be true that God, in Christ, is not counting my sin against me? Is it really true that, because of Jesus, and through faith in Him, my sin is gone, off the scorecard, thrown away? This absolutely sounds too good to be true, but Christ died for you and your sin. All of it, forever. Believe it, and thank God for it. Feel the tonnage of the burden of your sin lifted off of your back, and experience the freedom that is yours because Jesus credited it to you. Breathe in the clean air of deliverance.

The second common question is, "Does God really mean HIM?" We consider the most heinous acts of depravity, and we know that there are people who are simply too far gone. They have done too many sins that are too gross, and in too great a volume, to ever be forgiven by God. Yes, God really means them, too. Moses was a murderer, but God chose him. David was a sexual abuser and a murderer, but God made him into a man after His own heart. Saul dragged Christians from their homes and supervised their executions at the edge of town, but God saved him and turned him into the author of most of the New Testament books. There are hundreds of stories in the Bible just like theirs.

No one is beyond the reach of God's grace through Jesus. Not you. Not anyone.

PRAYER

God of all grace and comfort, I can barely take it in that I am free, and free forever. I pray that you will help me to never doubt my complete deliverance through Jesus, ever again. I also pray that you will help me to never doubt the power of Jesus to save even the worst person in the world, if there is one worse than me. Thank you, God! Amen.

REFLECTION QUESTIONS

- » Take a moment and imagine what it would feel like to never doubt God's love and forgiveness for you, ever again. Make this your goal.
- » Today, when you encounter mean people, make up a story that will help you forgive their actions. (They just found out they have cancer; their spouse just died; Something.) Then pray for God's grace to penetrate their lives.
- » Practice the memory verse.

TRUTH #24
WE ARE SAVED BY GRACE
THROUGH FAITH

QUOTE

"Faith is a living, daring confidence in God's grace, so sure and certain that a man could stake his life on it a thousand times."
- Martin Luther

SCRIPTURE

" And without faith it is impossible to please God, because anyone who comes to him must believe that he exists and that he rewards those who earnestly seek him."
- Hebrews 11:6

DEVOTIONAL

"What must I do to be saved?" This is the most important question in life. And what is the answer? Believe on the Lord Jesus and what He has done for you. The righteousness of God is given through faith in Jesus Christ to all who believe.

We were dead in our trespasses and sin. But because of His great love for us, God, who is rich in mercy, made us alive with Christ, even when we were dead in our transgressions and sin. Jesus did not come to make bad people good, He came to make dead people alive. He does so by His grace alone.

Jesus' grace is applied to your life by faith in Him, and the work He has done. Jesus changes everything for you, but if you don't possess the faith in Him to actually receive it, you will remain stuck in death while life awaits you. Faith is trusting that Jesus paid the penalty of your sin on your behalf, and that God will not seek to collect double payment by asking you to pay for what Jesus has already paid for you.

Not only does Jesus pay your penalty for you, and freely credit that payment to you, and then treat you forever as one who is as righteous as He, but He also gives you the faith it takes to actually receive it all. In other words, He supplies the grace, *and* He supplies the faith it takes to receive the grace. He does it all.

When Jesus went to the tomb of Lazarus, who had been dead for four days, and shouted, "Lazarus, come forth," notice that Lazarus did not march out of the tomb and high-five Jesus, saying, "What a great team we make, Jesus! Teamwork makes the dream work!" His resurrection was completely a work of God - and so is yours. "For it is by grace you have been saved, through faith—*and this is not from yourselves*, it is the gift of God— not by works, so that no one can boast." (Ephesians 2:8)

You have one job: Give grateful praise to God.

PRAYER

Merciful God, I renounce my pride and all thoughts of self-sufficiency, and I come to you in repentance and faith. I trust that your death gives me life. I praise you for the gift of salvation and for the gift of faith to receive that gift. Amen.

REFLECTION QUESTIONS

> » What is easier: to work really hard to earn God's love or to receive it by faith with no trust in your ability to deserve it?
> » How much blessing from God are you leaving sitting in the bank, just because you lack the faith to cash His check?
> » You were not just bad; you were dead. God isn't making you good; He is making you alive. What is the difference?
> » Practice the memory verse.

CONVERSATION 5 **WHAT IS THE GOSPEL?**

TRUTH #25
WE ARE JUSTIFIED AND ARE BEING SANCTIFIED

QUOTE

"I am not what I ought to be, I am not what I want to be, I am not what I hope to be in another world; but still I am not what I used to be, and by the grace of God I am what I am."
- John Newton

SCRIPTURE

"For those God foreknew he also predestined to be conformed to the image of his Son, that He might be the firstborn among many brothers and sisters. And those he predestined, he also called; those he called, he also justified; those he justified, he also glorified. What, then, shall we say in response to these things? If God is for us, who can be against us?"
- Romans 8:29-31

DEVOTIONAL

God decided some things about you long before you were a twinkle in your daddy's eye. God knew before the foundations of the world that you would respond to His gift of forgiveness in Jesus. Knowing you would respond, He predestined you, called you, justified you, and glorified you - all works of God by His grace, which you cannot earn. It breaks down like this:

He predestined (came to a decision beforehand) that you would be conformed to the image of Jesus. Notice "be conformed" and not "conform yourself." God decided beforehand to participate in your process of becoming "similar in form to the nature of" His Son. This way Jesus could be the firstborn of many brothers and sisters, who take on His nature and join the family.

He also called you: called you to join Him in this process of sanctification, and to join Christ in His mission in the world. Having called you, Christ justified you through His sacrifice on the cross, so God could see you "just as if I'd" never sinned before. Having justified you, in Christ, He also glorified you, in Christ, to be seated with Jesus in victory over all evil and enemies. To share in the fruit and freedom of His victory.

All of the finished work, He has done *for* you. And the ongoing, transforming work, He is doing **with** you. You are justified before God and are being sanctified. It is an ongoing process, involving cooperative work between you and the Holy Spirit, helping you to be conformed into the image of Jesus. God removes the fear of judgment so you can get on with the refining process of becoming like Jesus, your older brother and Lord. "For it is God who works in you, both to desire and to do His good purpose." (Philippians 2:13)

PRAYER

Gracious and loving Father, thank you for accomplishing the finished work of my redemption, and establishing my destiny, through Jesus, your Son. As I answer your call, please continue your transforming work in me and empower me to cooperate with your Holy Spirit in the process. I am free in You and being formed with You. I am your grateful child. Amen.

REFLECTION QUESTIONS

» How does it feel to recognize that God knew you before the foundations of the world?
» What part of the work on your behalf is already accomplished, and finished, through Jesus? Make a list and thank God for that list.
» What part of the transforming work is ongoing, as you work hard with the Spirit, for real change in your life? Commit to give God your all in this process of sanctification.
» Practice the memory verse.

CONVERSATION 5 DISCUSSION
WHAT IS THE GOSPEL?

Truth #21 All of Our Sins can be Forgiven
Truth #22 Jesus Reconciles All Things
Truth #23 The Grace of Jesus is Offered to All People
Truth #24 We are Saved by Grace Through Faith
Truth #25 We are Justified and are Being Sanctified

Gather with your Pursuit Group and have the following discussion:

- » Take turns reciting this Week's memory verse: 2 Timothy 1:9
- » How is the Pursuit going for you so far? How is God using it in your life?
- » What is harder for you - accepting God's forgiveness or forgiving yourself? Why?
- » Do you feel completely forgiven? How do you think your answer to the question affects your life?
- » What do you think people abuse most: Money, Sex, or Power? Why do you think that?
- » In which arena do you need to allow the gospel to have a greater influence on you: Power; Humility; Love; Money?
- » Did you try the "mean people" idea from Truth #23? How did it go?
- » How much blessing and goodness from God are you leaving untouched because you lack the faith to ask or receive?
- » What does it mean that we were dead in our sins and Christ made us alive? What does "dead" mean? What does "alive" mean?
- » How does it feel to know that God knew you before the foundations of the world?
- » What part of your ongoing sanctification (becoming more like Jesus) needs more progress lately? How happy are you with your overall progress? What is holding you back?
- » Share prayer requests and current life issues with one another.
- » Pray for each other.

CONVERSATION 6
HOW DOES GOD CONTINUE TO WORK IN ME?

WEEK 6 INTRODUCTION

When we meet Jesus and place our trust in Him, something happens that is so profound that the only way to describe it is like being born all over again; new birth that raises us from death to life! His Spirit bears witness with our spirit that we are His children. It is amazing, beautiful, and life-changing - 100% a work of God's grace!

Now, having become recipients of such amazing transformation, the process of walking daily with God, and letting the Spirit of Christ lead us and live through us begins. We offer ourselves as a living sacrifice to Him and He empowers and guides us, by His Spirit, to live powerful, free, and Kingdom-devoted lives. We learn to live in intimacy with God, intentionality with our families, and investment in His mission.

WEEK 6 MEMORY VERSE

 "Therefore, if anyone is in Christ, the new creation has come: The old has gone, the new is here!"

2 Corinthians 5:17

TRUTH #26
I AM BAPTIZED INTO THE BODY OF CHRIST

QUOTE

"Couldn't fight back the tears so I fell on my knees, saying, "God, if you're there come and rescue me." Felt love pouring down from above. Got washed in the water, washed in the blood, And now I'm changed. And now I'm stronger. There must be something in the water. Oh, there must be something in the water."
- Carrie Underwood, "Something in the Water"

SCRIPTURE

"We were therefore buried with him through baptism into death in order that, just as Christ was raised from the dead through the glory of the Father, we too may live a new life."
- Romans 6:4

DEVOTIONAL

After His resurrection, before He ascended into heaven, Jesus gave the disciples their marching orders, to "go and make disciples of all nations, baptizing them in the name of the Father, and of the Son and of the Holy Spirit, and teaching them to obey everything I have commanded you." (Matthew 28:19-20) Baptism in water is a baptism of repentance, and is the outward demonstration of our inward experience of being born into the family of God. Through our baptism, symbolized by our immersion in water, we are baptized into Christ and have clothed ourselves with Christ. (Galatians 3:27) We are found in Christ, not having any righteousness of our own, but that which comes through faith in Him.

Water baptism does not do this for us; it demonstrates that Christ has already done this in us.

Because of our baptism into Christ, we are no longer Jews or Gentiles, slaves or freed, or even males or females. We are all one in Christ Jesus and heirs according to His promise. (Galatians 3:28-29) We are one body and one Spirit, celebrating "one hope, one Lord, one faith, one baptism, one God and Father of all, who is over all and through all and in all." (Ephesians 4:5) We are one, together, in Him. Children of God, anchored into His family by His grace.

Your first step, after accepting salvation in Jesus, is to be baptized in water to publicly celebrate the work of Jesus in you. You are a child of God and a co-heir with Jesus. You are a part of the body of Christ and one with your brothers and sisters in Him. These profound realities are yours, and water baptism is your opportunity to celebrate them with your family, and to proclaim them to your friends who are far from God. It is to show the world what you already know inside: that you have been born again.

PRAYER

Thank you, God, for my new birth in Christ. Thank you for adopting me into your family and placing me in Him. Help me to find my identity in You and to celebrate my baptism into Christ, the death of the old life and the becoming new of all things. Amen.

REFLECTION QUESTIONS

- » What does water baptism symbolize?
- » Have you experienced God's Spirit bearing witness with you that you are His child? (if "yes," then celebrate that. If "no," then ask for Him to do this today)
- » What does it mean to be found in Christ?
- » What does it mean to be a joint-heir with Jesus?
- » Celebrate, as specifically as possible, what Jesus has done for you.
- » Practice the memory verse.

TRUTH #27
I AM OCCUPIED BY THE HOLY SPIRIT

QUOTE

"The Spirit is the empowering Presence of God for living the life of God every day."
- **Gordon D. Fee**

SCRIPTURE

"Those who are led by the Spirit of God are the children of God. The Spirit himself testifies with our spirit that we are God's children."
- **Romans 8:14-15**

DEVOTIONAL

Jesus said that He would not leave us as orphans, but that the Father would give us the Holy Spirit, who would be with us forever. He said that the Spirit would live *with* us and be *in* us. (John 14) If you have received Christ, you have received the Holy Spirit. If you do not have the Holy Spirit, you do not have Christ. (Romans 8) This is profoundly and fundamentally important, for not only are you never, ever alone, but your body is now and always filled with the Presence and Power of God Himself.

What a game changer! The same Spirit that raised Christ Jesus from the dead and gave life to His mortal body, lives in you. He gives you comfort, guidance, strength, and peace. He gives you power to live your life fully submitted to God, and to walk in victory over all the forces of evil in the world. He is the down payment for what you will more fully enjoy in Heaven.

The Spirit's Presence brings fruit into your life; love, joy, peace, gentleness, kindness, patience, faithfulness, and self-control. We enjoy this fruit in real time as we lean into His Presence and allow Him to live through us.

Mary was told she would be made pregnant with the Son of God because "The Holy Spirit will come on you, and the power of the Most High will overshadow you. So the holy one to be born will be called the Son of God." (Luke 1:35) In much the same way, God now fills us with the Holy Spirit and the power of the Most High dwells in us. This makes us pregnant with the supernatural, so that the life we live in this fallen world will be called a work of God! As Mary bore the very literal fruit of the newborn Messiah, you will bear the fruit of the Spirit in your own life. You can be sure, it is a blessing very much like the one bestowed upon Mary.

PRAYER

Oh God, my Father, I bow my knees to declare that I am a servant of the Most High God. I lift up my hands and pray, Come, Holy Spirit, and fill me this day that I might glorify Jesus. Amen.

REFLECTION QUESTIONS

- » How can you lean into the Spirit's Presence in you today?
- » What keeps you from recognizing His Presence throughout your day or in times of trouble?
- » How different would your life be if you trusted for and expected the Holy Spirit within you every day?
- » Practice the memory verse.

TRUTH #28
I MUST PARTICIPATE IN MY
ONGOING TRANSFORMATION

QUOTE

"Spiritual formation prepares us for a life in which we move away from our fears, compulsions, resentments, and sorrows, to serve with joy and courage in the world, even when this leads us to places we would rather not go. Spiritual formation helps us to see the face of God in the midst of a hardened world and in our own heart."
- Henri J. M. Nouwen

SCRIPTURE

"Work out your salvation with fear and trembling, for it is God who works in you to will and to act in order to fulfill his good purpose."
- Philippians 2:13

DEVOTIONAL

The things I don't want to do, I keep on doing; the things I want to do, I don't do. Wretched man that I am, who can save me from this treadmill of failure and inner-turmoil? We all know what it's like to feel this way, but, thanks be to God, through Jesus Christ our Lord; we can overcome.

Remember, we are not human *doings*, we are human *beings*, and, even more accurately, we are eternal *spiritual* beings. The ongoing journey of becoming more like Jesus is a journey of spiritual formation, where the work of God accomplished for you, and the Spirit's Presence in you, empower you to participate in the formation of a new person. This person trades your hate for love, your sorrow for joy, your anxiety for peace, your aggression for gentleness, your meanness for kindness, your irritability for patience, your selfishness for faithfulness, and your instability for self-control. It is God who works in you to both desire and to do His good pleasure. He works in you, gives you His desires for your heart, and empowers you to act upon it all.

Most of us think that success over our sin would mean that we no longer desire sin, or find it attractive. Or that success over our anger is to never feel anger again, etc. That is naive. Victory is not the absence of struggle; victory is overcoming the struggle and living with freedom inside the struggle. Victory is having your mind governed by the Spirit, rather than your flesh, and crying out to God, your Father, when your flesh is screaming for earthly satisfaction.

Be encouraged; as you plant the Word of God into your heart, as you pursue intimacy with God in prayer, and as you lean into the work of the Spirit inside you, you will not be as good at sin as you once were, and Christlikeness will become a more and more common experience. You will find that you are increasingly acting like the person God already says you are.

PRAYER

Almighty God of grace and patience, please work *in* me what you have already done *for* me. Help me to hunger and thirst for you and for your Word, that I might be transformed by the renewing of my mind. Help me to daily surrender to your leadership in my life and to know that I am more than a conqueror through You who strengthens me. Amen.

REFLECTION QUESTIONS

» Reflect on how much your life has changed since you started following Jesus. If you are new to faith, daydream for a minute on how much change can come to your life this year.
» Why is it important to know that victory does not mean the absence of struggle?
» What new spiritual discipline could you begin to regularly practice, to increase your spiritual strength and endurance? (make a small, daily goal)
» Practice the memory verse.

TRUTH #29
GOD HAS PLACED ME ON
MISSION WITH HIM

QUOTE

*"Christ has no body now but yours. No hands, no feet on
earth but yours. Yours are the eyes through which he looks
with compassion on this world. Yours are the feet with which
he walks to do good. Yours are the hands through which he
blesses all the world. Christ has no body now on earth but
yours."*
- **Teresa of Avila**

SCRIPTURE

*"Believe in the Lord Jesus, and you will be saved—you and
your household."*
- **Acts 16:31**

DEVOTIONAL

One day Jesus delivered, healed, and completely transformed a
man tormented by a legion of demons. He lived naked among the
tombs, cutting himself with rocks and terrifying the city. The guy
was so grateful for what Jesus did for him that he wanted to travel
with Him wherever He went. What a great miracle story Jesus could
use to draw big crowds and wow audiences. But Jesus refused and
told him, instead, to "go back to your own people and tell them
everything the Lord has done for you." (Mark 5:19)

Jesus knew a secret that this man did not yet understand.

Like that man, your life has been changed by God's grace and you
want to glorify Him and serve Him. Maybe you have ideas about what
that might look like, but Jesus knows a secret that *you* might not yet
understand.

The secret is that you were created on purpose and made for a
mission; He pulled you out of darkness in order to send you back
into that darkness, to help others find their way back to God too.
The secret is that you are the best candidate possible to love, serve,

and influence certain people. Those people are called, in the Bible, your "oikos" or "household." These are your family, neighbors, co-workers, friends, and those within your traffic pattern, in whose lives you already have influence and favor. He has already, strategically and supernaturally, placed a group of people in your world as your personal assignment. Going to foreign countries is awesome, but it is not the best way to find your personal mission. You are living in it right now.

The Roman jailer in Acts 16, Cornelius in Acts 11, Zacchaeus in Luke 19, and the woman at the well in John 4 all used their transformation story to influence their Oikos toward Jesus and were used by God to help them find their way back to Him. This is the way God has chosen to change the world; using transformed people to introduce their Oikos to God so He can change their world too. He is changing the world, one household at a time, and He wants to use you to change your world, too.

PRAYER

Thank you, Jesus, for turning my life right-side up. You have changed everything for me. Help me to join you in mission to my Oikos. Help me to love them as you do, share my story with them, and cover them with my prayers. Here am I, send me. Amen.

REFLECTION QUESTIONS

- » Give thanks to God for the specific things He has done for you.
- » Make a list of the top 10 people with whom you have the most influence.
- » Pray for those 10 people and watch for opportunities to serve them well.
- » Practice the memory verse.

CONVERSATION 6 **HOW DOES GOD CONTINUE TO WORK IN ME?**

TRUTH #30
I CAN ENJOY ETERNAL LIFE
TODAY

QUOTE

"What were we made for? To know God. What aim should we have in life? To know God. What is the eternal life that Jesus gives? To know God. What is the best thing in life? To know God. What in us gives God most pleasure? Knowledge of himself."
- J. I. Packer

SCRIPTURE

"Now this is eternal life: that they know you, the only true God, and Jesus Christ, whom you have sent."
- John 17:3

DEVOTIONAL

One day, God will wrap up this world and introduce us to our eternal destiny. What an awesome and unimaginable thing that will be! But eternal life is not only life in eternity, it is also an eternal kind of life that can be lived right now. An eternal quality of life that can be enjoyed today in spite of our fallen state, and one that will be enjoyed without limit in eternity.

When your body dies, you will not cease to exist. In a nanosecond you will walk out of this life and into the next one. You will never die. In fact, your eternal life in God's Kingdom has already begun. As D. L. Moody famously said, "Someday you will read or hear that Dwight Moody is dead. Don't you believe a word of it. I shall be more alive than I am now. I will just have changed my address. I will have gone into the presence of God." Eternal life is not only something to look forward to, but also to be lived right here and right now.

This is enormously important because it enables us to experience absurd happiness and complete fearlessness in this life, even while being constantly challenged. Knowing God is eternal life; to walk with Him, enjoy His Presence, and be protected by His strength; to know our Abba, Father. Abba is the Hebrew word which most embodies the notion of "daddy," and Jesus taught us to know God intimately, to refer to Him this way when we pray. He, Himself, cried out to His Abba on the night before His death. Knowing our Abba, Father, is eternal life, and knowing Him is only possible through Jesus.

Jesus said, "whoever drinks the water I give them will never thirst. Indeed, the water I give them will become in them a spring of water welling up to eternal life." (John 4:14) Eternal life is found in Jesus, and when Jesus finds you, He places in you the fountain of eternal life that enables you to never thirst again - in this life or the next.

PRAYER

Abba, Father, thank you for adopting me into your family and making me your child. Knowing you is eternal life and I ask you to well up in me the eternal kind of life today. Help me this day to be, in you, absurdly happy and completely fearless - like I will be every day in eternity. Amen.

REFLECTION QUESTIONS

» How far are you from absurd happiness and complete fearlessness? Why?
» What comes to your mind as you imagine living an eternal quality of life today?
» Imagine God being the ultimate Father, embracing you with tenderness and strength. Rest there for a minute.
» Practice the memory verse.

CONVERSATION 6 DISCUSSION
HOW DOES GOD CONTINUE TO
WORK IN ME?

Truth #26 I am Baptized Into the Body of Christ
Truth #27 I Am Occupied by the Holy Spirit
Truth #28 I Must Participate in My Ongoing Transformation
Truth #29 I Was Made for a Mission
Truth #30 I Can Enjoy Eternal Life Today

Gather with your Pursuit Group and have the following discussion:

- » Take turns reciting this Week's memory verse: 2 Corinthians 5:17
- » How important is water baptism? Was yours a significant event in your life? Why or why not?
- » In what ways do you typically experience the Presence of God's Spirit?
- » What does it mean to be "in Christ"?
- » What does it mean to be a joint-heir with Jesus?
- » How different would your life be if you trusted for and expected Mary Miracles every day?
- » What does victory over your struggles look like for you?
- » What spiritual disciplines have you tried? What has worked well for you?
- » What is one way you could grow your spiritual strength and endurance?
- » Which persons in your Oikos need you the most right now?
- » On a scale of 1-10, how much do you experience absurd happiness and complete fearlessness? Why?
- » How much do you experience God as your Abba, Father? Explain.
- » Share prayer requests and current life issues with one another.
- » Pray for each other.

CONVERSATION 7
WHAT IS THE CHURCH?

WEEK 7 INTRODUCTION

What is the Church? Is it a building you go to? Is it an organization that provides goods and services for Christians to consume? Is it a non-profit, humanitarian organization that exists to serve broken people? Is it a holy space where God lives and people can come to be with Him? Does it exist for itself or entirely for others? Or is it altogether something else? Throughout history, people have had all of these views of church, and more, but maybe we should let God define it, since it was His idea in the first place.

WEEK 7 MEMORY VERSE

"His intent was that now, through the church, the manifold wisdom of God should be made known to the rulers and authorities in the heavenly realms, according to his eternal purpose that he accomplished in Christ Jesus our Lord."

Ephesians 3:10-11

TRUTH #31
WE ARE THE CALLED-OUT ONES

QUOTE

"She say, Celie, tell the truth, have you ever found God in church? I never did. I just found a bunch of folks hoping for him to show. Any God I ever felt in church I brought in with me. And I think all the other folks did too. They come to church to share God, not to find God."
- Alice Walker (The Color Purple)

SCRIPTURE

"On this rock I will build my church, and the gates of Hell will not overcome it. I will give you the keys of the kingdom of heaven; whatever you bind on earth will be bound in heaven, and whatever you loose on earth will be loosed in heaven."
- Matthew 16:18-19

DEVOTIONAL

Jesus is the One who created the concept of the church, and it is He that gets to define it. The Greek word He chose is eklesia, from two words: ek = out of, and kaleo = to call. The Church is the "called out ones." The people of God, called out of their sin, death, and broken world, that they might belong to God and be His body for the world to see. God's people don't go to church; they *are* the church.

God calls His people to come out of the darkness and into the light, and be one together in Him. We leave our addiction to the pleasures, promises, and provisions of this world, and give ourselves fully to Christ and His Kingdom. We are built together to become a dwelling in which God lives by His Spirit. We are His people who become His body, doing His work of destroying the gates of darkness so others can find God through us. Wherever two or three of us are gathered, there He is in our midst. We are given the keys of His Kingdom, and are entrusted with His power to bind and loose evil and goodness in this world.

We are called out, and sent back in.

How many churches are there in your city? The answer is, One. How many churches are there in the entire world? Only one. We meet in

CONVERSATION 7   **WHAT IS THE CHURCH?**

various buildings, and unite around various distinctives, but together, we are one body, living out one faith in one Lord, united together through one baptism. I currently serve as the Pastor of the portion of the church that meets at Evergreen. If you are a member of Evergreen, you are a part of His church that gathers here. Evergreen is not the church - it is a place where a portion of the church gathers.

The church is not a place, it is a people. Together we are a habitation of God by His Spirit and His actual hands and feet on this earth. This is 100% a work of God that we are not qualified for, nor could we ever accomplish on our own. Yet it is another gift from our incredible God.

PRAYER

God, you have called me out of darkness to become one with your people- the church. Thank you for living in me, and for living in us. Help me to be a healthy part of your body, that your church can represent you and your Kingdom well. Make us one in you so that all people may know your greatness and love. Amen.

REFLECTION QUESTIONS

- » What is the church?
- » The smallest church is the family. How is your church (family) doing at being the body of Jesus?
- » Decide right now to practice being the church in your world today. How might you do that?
- » Practice the memory verse.

_____

_____

_____

_____

_____

_____

_____

_____

_____

_____

TRUTH #32
WE ARE THE PEOPLE OF GOD'S PRESENCE

QUOTE

"We (Christians) are always in the presence of God. There is never a non-sacred moment! His presence never diminishes. Our awareness of His presence may falter, but the reality of His presence never changes."
- **Max Lucado**

SCRIPTURE

"And I will ask the Father, and he will give you another Helper, to be with you forever, even the Spirit of truth, whom the world cannot receive, because it neither sees him nor knows him. You know him, for he dwells with you and will be in you."
- **John 14:16-17**

DEVOTIONAL

I've always been struck by Jesus' words: "Apart from me you can do nothing." They are a humbling and refreshing reminder that our need, from first to last, isn't partial, but total. By giving us the Holy Spirit, Christ has given us Himself. Our bodies become houses where God lives, and His Presence becomes the source of our daily obedience, fruitfulness, and love. This is the wisdom of God, "a mystery that has been hidden and that God destined for our glory before time began. None of the rulers of this age understood it, for if they had, they would have never crucified the Lord of glory." (1 Corinthians 2:7-8)

When Jesus rose from the dead, the Kingdom of God inverted itself and went from being contained in the person of Jesus, to being unleashed into the bodies of every person whom Christ redeems, through the occupancy of the Spirit in them. If the rulers of darkness had understood this, they would have never let Jesus get to that cross!

Now His people are carriers of the divine Presence, and the Presence of God means that nothing is impossible. Why? The Presence of

God has come. He is here, right now, wherever you are. Whether you remain aware of it or not, He is wherever you are *all the time*.

"You will receive power when the Holy Spirit comes upon you and you shall be my witnesses." (Acts 1:8) The word, "witnesses" is the Greek word, "martyrion" where we get the word martyr. The Presence of God enables us to die to ourselves and live for God. It makes my life verse, Galatians 2:20, an absolute reality: "I am crucified with Christ, nevertheless I live. Not I, but Christ lives in me and the life I now live in the body, I live by faith in the Son of God who loved me and gave Himself for me."

PRAYER

Thank you, Father, for your Presence in my life through the Holy Spirit. Help me to remain aware of your nearness and lean into your power - the power to die to myself and live for you. May I be the fragrance of Christ to you this day. Amen.

REFLECTION QUESTIONS

- » Think about all the things that could happen if Jesus were physically walking with you everywhere you go. Now, realize that He actually is and open your mind to believing for more.
- » When you are alone today, driving or whatever, consciously quiet your mind and ask the Spirit to speak to you. Listen carefully and write down whatever comes to mind.
- » Practice the memory verse.

TRUTH #33
WE ARE CITIZENS OF GOD'S KINGDOM

QUOTE

"It is not what we do that matters, but what a sovereign God chooses to do through us. God doesn't want our success; He wants us. He doesn't demand our achievements; He demands our obedience. The Kingdom of God is a kingdom of paradox, where through the ugly defeat of a cross, a holy God is utterly glorified. Victory comes through defeat; healing through brokenness; finding self through losing self."
- Charles Colson

SCRIPTURE

"But our citizenship is in heaven. And we eagerly await a Savior from there, the Lord Jesus Christ."
- Philippians 3:20

DEVOTIONAL

Jesus' ministry on earth was dominated by one primary message: "Repent, for the Kingdom of Heaven has come near." (Matthew 4:17) The Kingdom is mentioned 126 times in the gospels, yet it is not simply defined anywhere in the New Testament. However, the Kingdom of God, as a concept was very familiar to the Jewish people. It had been told to them, by prophets and by God Himself, that "...the God of heaven will set up a kingdom that shall never be destroyed." (Daniel 2:44) This was the role they expected Jesus to play, as a conquering King, and is why many of them did not accept Jesus as the Messiah.

Rather than bringing war and conquering the Roman empire, Jesus demonstrated God's Kingdom by showing God's power to heal the sick, open blind eyes, dominate evil, and strengthen the poor. He not only announced the Kingdom, but showed that this was a Kingdom of the Spirit; one that crosses all earthly borders. He modeled Kingdom values and demonstrated Kingdom power so all could see. He pulled back the curtain on the Kingdom of God and invited us to enter into that Kingdom right now.

In Matthew chapter six, when He taught us how to pray, Jesus' model prayer encourages us to make this request of God: "may your Kingdom come, and your will be done, on earth just as it is in Heaven." The literal translation of that part of the prayer is, "Come, Your Kingdom! Be done, Your will! On earth just like it is in Heaven." In other words, He taught us to call the Kingdom of God into our space, and command that the will of God find expression right here, right now - just like it does in Heaven.

In Christ we have citizenship in the Kingdom of Heaven, with all of its privileges and responsibilities. We are to demonstrate the Kingdom of God with our lives as He did - by modeling Kingdom values, demonstrating Kingdom power, and fixing our eyes on the full expression of His Kingdom every day. The Kingdom of God has come!

PRAYER

King of all kings and Lord of all lords, thank you for invading our space with your Presence and power! Thank you for showing us the Kingdom and for making life in the Kingdom possible for me now and forever. Help me to seek your Kingdom first, every day of my life, and to allow you to demonstrate your Kingdom rule through my life. Amen.

REFLECTION QUESTIONS

» Why is repentance attached to the arrival of God's Kingdom? When is the last time you repented for your sin? Maybe it's time to do so again and maintain a posture of repentance.

» Just as sin invaded the Garden of Eden, now God's Kingdom invades our fallen world. How can you participate in this Kingdom invasion today? Be specific.

» What do you seek most in life? What will it take for you to seek God's Kingdom more than you seek anything else? Is that even possible?

» Practice the memory verse.

TRUTH #34
WE ARE A PROPHETIC VOICE TO THE CULTURE

QUOTE

"If your Gospel isn't touching others, it hasn't touched you!"
- **Curry R. Blake**

SCRIPTURE

"Do not conform to the pattern of this world."
- **Romans 12:2**

DEVOTIONAL

God has always longed for a people for Himself - His people - who walk with Him, trust Him fully, and live in His Kingdom. In both the Old and New Testaments, God established covenants in order to form a people for Himself, who are distinguished from all other people on the earth. What distinguishes them is both their obedience to the One True God, and their living in full engagement with His mission in the world. That mission is to have His glory cover the earth as the waters cover the sea.

God's people distinguish themselves by living like no one else. They find their life by losing it. They become the greatest by becoming the servant of all. They love their enemies, and pray for those who persecute them. They love one another with a love that publicly proclaims their connection to God. They live in, and for, a Kingdom that the world cannot see. It is this covenant life that empowers them to experience joy, peace, provision, and true human fulfillment like no one else.

Their culture, values, unity, and compassion make them a prophetic voice for God. Theirs is a counter-culture designed to be both their source of God's favor and their prophetic witness to a lost world. They care for the widow, the orphan, the poor, and the vulnerable. They carry God's burden for the elimination of injustice, and they sacrifice joyfully for others who could never repay them.

Like an unstoppable force that meets an immovable object, the kingdoms collide, and the people of God find themselves on the outs with their modern culture. While this collision often ends in hostility toward God's people, they respond with grace, seeking the prosperity of the nation in which they are in exile. They share in the sufferings of Jesus that they may also share in His resurrection.

PRAYER

God of all grace, I know you love the whole world the way you love me. It is your desire to see all people find their way back to you and for your glory to cover the earth. Help me to live my life the way you desire to live it through me. Let me be a prophetic voice for you today, helping the world sense your Presence and know your love. Amen.

REFLECTION QUESTIONS

- » What is the greatest cause of atheism in the world today?
- » How effectively are you living your life as a prophetic voice to the world?
- » How can your life speak for God today?
- » Practice the memory verse.

TRUTH #35
WE SERVE ONE OBJECTIVE - THE GLORY OF GOD

QUOTE

"The greatest single cause of atheism in the world today is Christians, who acknowledge Jesus with their lips and walk out the door and deny Him by their lifestyle. That is what an unbelieving world simply finds unbelievable."
- Brennan Manning

SCRIPTURE

"The Spirit of the Lord is on me, because he has anointed me to proclaim good news to the poor. He has sent me to proclaim freedom for the prisoners and recovery of sight for the blind, to set the oppressed free, to proclaim the year of the Lord's favor."
- Luke 4:18-19

DEVOTIONAL

All of creation - the heavens, the galaxies, the land and sea, and all that dwell in them - we all exist for one purpose: the Glory of God. When a created thing functions in the way it was designed, it is a beautiful thing. Conversely, when a created thing attempts to function in a way for which it was not designed, it is at best awkward, and at worst disastrous. Everything wrong in the world is the fruit of man's ignorance, rebellion, and refusal to submit to his Sovereign Designer.

But God's glory cannot be stopped! It is the glory of God to satisfy the demands of justice and extend mercy to the rebel, both through the sacrifice of Himself. Then we, who are the redeemed people of God, return to fulfill our original purpose - the Glory of God. We do so by joining Jesus in the redemptive work of drawing rebels back to God, and righting the wrongs we have created. We do this through the Spirit of God who has been given to us. He anoints us to proclaim God's goodness.

What is the primary work of the anointed? To proclaim good news to the poor and the prisoner; to restore sight to the blind, to set the oppressed free, and to proclaim the favor of God for the redeemed. This is the glory of God - to forgive, to restore, and to set free. We take the same mindset as Jesus, "Who, being in very nature God, did not consider equality with God something to be used to his own advantage; rather, he made himself nothing by taking the very nature of a servant." (Philippians 2:6-7)

We are a Kingdom of servants, willing to give our all so that our King may be glorified. The Spirit of our King works in us to be made into the likeness of our King so we can serve the mission of our King, for the glory of our King. This is our single purpose and the pathway to our greatest pleasure.

PRAYER

King of all kings, I praise you this day and ask you to anoint me with your Spirit so that I may be conformed into your image and serve your mission. Help me to trust you so much that I gladly give my whole self to the purpose of bringing you glory. Guide me to the people I can best serve for you today, and then do your work through me, for your glory and not my own. Amen.

REFLECTION QUESTIONS

- » What is your purpose in life?
- » Reflect on your various roles (child, spouse, parent, worker, friend, neighbor, etc). Think of how to fulfill your purpose in at least two of those roles.
- » Decide today that you will live for one primary objective - the glory of God.
- » Practice the memory verse.

CONVERSATION 7 DISCUSSION
WHAT IS THE CHURCH?

Truth #31 We are the Called-Out Ones
Truth #32 We are the People of God's Presence
Truth #33 We are Citizens of God's Kingdom
Truth #34 We are a Prophetic Voice to the Culture
Truth #35 We Serve One Objective - The Glory of God

Gather with your Pursuit Group and have the following discussion:

- » Take turns reciting this Week's memory verse: Ephesians 3:10-11
- » What is the Church?
- » How can we practice being the Church in our world?
- » If Jesus spent a week, physically beside you, how would you use Him?
- » When you quiet your mind and ask God to speak to you, what happens? Any success?
- » Why is repentance the first step into the Kingdom of God?
- » How does God's Kingdom invade our world today? How can you participate in this invasion? (list at least 5 ways)
- » What do you most want out of life? (be honest, simple, and specific)
- » How would seeking God's Kingdom first affect that list?
- » To what extent do you really believe that if you seek God's Kingdom first, everything you need will be taken care of?
- » How can your life serve as a prophetic voice for God? (Prophetic = to express God's heart in a particular moment for that moment)
- » Pick one role you have in life: How could you do that role in a way that better glorifies God?
- » Share prayer requests and current life issues with one another.
- » Pray for each other.

CONVERSATION 8
HOW IS IT ALL GOING TO END?

WEEK 8 INTRODUCTION

The Garden of Eden is a glimpse into what God had in mind when He created the world. There was beauty and balance in creation; man, planet, and beast lived in harmony; humans enjoyed intimacy with God and with one another. There was work and purpose for man as he bore the image of God in dominion over creation.

But the garden became contaminated, and the rest of history is the story of God's response to paradise lost. Jesus, whose crucifixion was established before the foundations of the world, will bring a dramatic ending to the story with a decisive victory, a final judgment day, and the introduction of a new heaven and new earth. Paradise will be restored, and God will be glorified forever, as His redeemed ones live their destiny in their eternal home, while those who reject God will suffer His absence forever in theirs.

WEEK 8 MEMORY VERSE

"Look, I am coming soon! My reward is with me, and I will give to each person according to what they have done. I am the Alpha and the Omega, the First and the Last, the Beginning and the End."

Revelation 22:12-13

TRUTH #36
CHRIST WILL RETURN AGAIN

QUOTE

"When He returns is not as important as the fact that we are ready for Him when He does return."
A. W. Tozer

SCRIPTURE

"Do not let your hearts be troubled. You believe in God; believe also in me. My Father's house has many rooms; if that were not so, would I have told you that I am going there to prepare a place for you? And if I go and prepare a place for you, I will come back and take you to be with me that you also may be where I am."
John 14:1-3

DEVOTIONAL

When Jesus ascended, He proved that He rules over death and now occupies His throne of authority over everything. He defeated death for everyone so that we need never again give way to fear. We live in confidence because our King has won the war and will soon return to complete His victory over evil. Just as the defining battle of a conflict may be won long before the final victory, so too do we live in the victory of Christ while still awaiting the resolution of the war.

The second coming of Jesus initiates the final conflict and opens the next chapter of the God-story. His throne will be established on the earth for 1,000 years, and then, in an epic battle, the powers of Hell will be soundly defeated, exiled to Hell forever. It all begins with those who have died in Christ being caught up in the air together with those who are alive and remain until the coming of the Lord. (1 Thessalonians 4:16, 17; Romans 8:23; Titus 2:13; 1 Corinthians 15:51,52)

His second coming will be literal, physical, and visible. The Bible emphasizes that it will happen suddenly without warning and that believers should remain in a state of continual readiness. (Philippians 4:5; Hebrews 10:37; James 5:8, 9; Revelation 22:10)

While there is great debate about the details of how this will all unfold, one thing is crystal clear: if we are in Christ, we win! In fact, the war is already won, so we wait in eager anticipation for His return and the consummation of our new future. In the meantime, we are to "live self-controlled, upright and godly lives in this present age, while we wait for the blessed hope—the appearing of the glory of our great God and Savior, Jesus Christ." (Titus 2:12-13)

PRAYER

Risen and Ascended Lord, though you no longer walk this earth, you rule over us from your throne. All authority and power are in you. Your name is above all names. Help me live in eager anticipation of your final victory and the fact that you will raise me up at the last day to live with you in your kingdom. Amen.

REFLECTION QUESTIONS

» Are you eager for the return of Jesus? Why or why not?
» How does knowing that the outcome of the war is already determined help you choose peace in the middle of your current battle?
» Read Revelation 22:1-14 and thank God for what is coming soon.
» Practice the memory verse.

TRUTH #37
EVERY PERSON WILL GIVE AN ACCOUNT TO GOD

QUOTE

"Do not be afraid of those who kill the body but cannot kill the soul. Instead, fear the One who can destroy both soul and body in hell."
- **Jesus**

SCRIPTURE

"And I saw the dead, great and small, standing before the throne, and books were opened. Another book was opened, which is the book of life. The dead were judged according to what they had done as recorded in the books."
- **Revelation 20:12**

DEVOTIONAL

Jesus was clear: there will come a day when God will judge the living and the dead and will separate them for heaven and for hell. Matthew 25, as only one example, is an entire chapter on the certainty of that day of judgment. As terrifying as that sounds, and it absolutely is, He was also clear that you can be ready for it now and live in a state of readiness with joy and peace.

See, the final judgment will not be based on your deeds, but on your wardrobe.

In Matthew 22, Jesus told a parable where a King prepared a wedding feast for His Son and invited all of His guests. However, when it was time for the banquet, they all had lame excuses and declined to attend; their busy lives were more important to them than the King's Son. The King made a new plan to fill the banquet so His Son would be honored: "So the servants went out into the streets and gathered all the people they could find, *the bad as well as the good,* and the wedding hall was filled with guests."

Once the hall was full, the King noticed that there was one wedding guest who was not wearing wedding clothes. He erupted in outrage and asked, 'How did you get in here without wedding clothes, friend?' The man was speechless. Then the king told the attendants, 'Tie him hand and foot, and throw him outside, into the darkness, where there will be weeping and gnashing of teeth." (This was a description Jesus frequently used for Hell.)

What qualifies you for Heaven is not your deeds. On that basis, everyone is hopeless and deserves death. What qualifies you for Heaven is being clothed in the righteousness of Jesus, by faith in His sacrifice and resurrection. To be clothed with Christ, being otherwise naked in your sin and shame without merit. Jesus is making it clear that His Kingdom makes room for everyone, but that proper attire is required.

PRAYER

King of all creation, make me mindful that one day I will stand before you for judgment. Thank you for saving me from the outcome I deserve. Help me be faithful to encourage others to flee from the wrath to come. I look in hope to the joy that will be mine when, clothed with the merits of Jesus, I will be saved from that wrath and invited to reign with Him on a renewed earth. Amen.

REFLECTION QUESTIONS

- » Are you personally able to live in perpetual peace about the day of judgment? Why or why not?
- » What is the most difficult part of the concept of eternal judgment for you to get your arms around? Why?
- » If it is not about the deeds we have done, why are our deeds recorded in the books? (hint: see Truth #13)
- » Practice the memory verse.

TRUTH #38
HELL IS THE ETERNAL HOME FOR THOSE WHO REJECT GOD

QUOTE

"Those who go to Heaven ride on a pass and enter into blessings that they never earned, but all who go to hell pay their own way."
- **John R. Rice**

SCRIPTURE

"Then they will go away to eternal punishment, but the righteous to eternal life."
- **Jesus, Matthew 25:46**

DEVOTIONAL

The reality of Hell is the most difficult and controversial of all Christian beliefs. Even those who are fully devoted to Jesus struggle to imagine an eternal destiny of damnation for any, having tasted the kindness and mercy of God for themselves. How can the God who loves the entire world possibly send a large portion of the world into an eternal Hell?

This line of reasoning focuses accusingly on the character of God, and not at all on the character of the condemned. Personally, I have little trouble embracing the idea of punishment for injustice. I more struggle to understand why God does not damn us all. The shocker is not that some people will end up in Hell, it is that not everyone will. His gracious invitation to eternal life is extended to all, for the Son of man did not come into the world to condemn it, but that, through Him, the world might be saved. (John 3:17)

What exactly is Hell? It is a place completely void of the Presence and goodness of God, where no one bows to His authority or embraces His grace. Anywhere this reality exists, there will certainly be weeping and gnashing of teeth, and the only way to end up there is to reject God: reject His authority, reject His gracious suffering for your sin, and refuse to bow your knee to His rule.

You only end up in Hell if you exercise the free will God graciously allotted to you by choosing to have nothing to do with Him. In other words, if you end up in Hell it is because that is precisely what you chose - a place without the rule of God. You will have gotten what your self-absorbed sins deserved and your rebellious heart desired.

PRAYER

Holy and perfect God of justice. Thank you for pouring grace and mercy upon me, to reveal your glory as the God who redeems at great personal cost. May I live in constant gratitude for Christ with my knees perpetually bowed before your throne. You are worthy and I am grateful. Amen.

REFLECTION QUESTIONS

» Is the idea of eternal punishment for sin difficult for you? Why or why not?
» Who ends up in Hell?
» Why is it possible to know that your eternal destiny is heaven?
» Practice the memory verse.

CONVERSATION 8 **HOW IS IT ALL GOING TO END?**

TRUTH #39
HEAVEN IS PREPARED FOR THE REDEEMED

QUOTE

"Joy is the serious business of Heaven."
- **C. S. Lewis**

SCRIPTURE

"Then I saw a new heaven and a new earth, for the first heaven and the first earth had passed away, and the sea was no more. And I saw the holy city, new Jerusalem, coming down out of heaven from God, prepared as a bride adorned for her husband. And I heard a loud voice from the throne saying, "Behold, the dwelling place of God is with man. He will dwell with them, and they will be his people, and God himself will be with them as their God. He will wipe away every tear from their eyes, and death shall be no more, neither shall there be mourning, nor crying, nor pain anymore, for the former things have passed away."
- **Revelation 21:1-4**

DEVOTIONAL

Jesus promised that He was going to heaven to prepare a place for us and that, once prepared, He would return to take us there Himself. Heaven is the environment and the experience that our souls achingly long for. In our spiritual DNA is the memory of the Paradise of Eden and our soul can find no rest until it finds its rest in God.

Read again the description given to John in Revelation 21: "They will be his people, and God himself will be with them and be their God. 'He will wipe every tear from their eyes. There will be no more death' or mourning or crying or pain, for the old order of things has passed away.'" My favorite part? "God himself will be with them." Wow!

Heaven is the place where we will enjoy the Presence of God without filter or limit. There will be no need of the sun, moon, or stars, for the glory of God will light up the sky. No death, sorrow, mourning, or pain. It will be life exactly how God intended it. Our mortal bodies will put on immortality, and we will enjoy both the Presence of God, and the absence of evil, forever!

Forget about images of angels on clouds, playing harps. Don't think of heaven as an eternal church worship service. As one of my all-time favorite songs says, "One of these days, I'm gonna see the hands that took the nails for me. One of these days, I'm gonna hold the key to the mansion built for me. One of these days I'm gonna walk the streets of gold that were paved for me. One of these days I'm gonna see my Savior face-to-face. One of these days." I just can't wait!

PRAYER

Eternal and glorious God, I eagerly anticipate joining you in your kingdom. I long for the day when you will dry every tear with your own hand. I long for my battle with my flesh to be finally won. Let the sure hope of everlasting life give me courage to face the trials of this life. Amen. Come, Lord Jesus!

REFLECTION QUESTIONS

- » What do you anticipate most about Heaven? What will be the best part?
- » If you get to ask God one question when you first arrive, what will you ask?
- » What is one question you have about Heaven? Ask God and listen for an answer.
- » Practice the memory verse.

TRUTH #40
THERE WILL BE A NEW HEAVEN AND A NEW EARTH

QUOTE

"Most people, if they had really learned to look into their own hearts, would know that they do want, and want acutely, something that cannot be had in this world. There are all sorts of things in this world that offer to give it to you, but they never quite keep their promise. . . . If we find ourselves with a desire that nothing in this world can satisfy, the most probable explanation is that we were made for another world."
- C. S. Lewis

SCRIPTURE

"Then the angel showed me the river of the water of life, as clear as crystal, flowing from the throne of God and of the Lamb down the middle of the great street of the city. On each side of the river stood the tree of life, bearing twelve crops of fruit, yielding its fruit every month. And the leaves of the tree are for the healing of the nations. No longer will there be any curse. The throne of God and of the Lamb will be in the city, and his servants will serve him. They will see his face, and his name will be on their foreheads. There will be no more night. They will not need the light of a lamp or the light of the sun, for the Lord God will give them light. And they will reign for ever and ever."
- Revelation 22:1-5

DEVOTIONAL

What John saw in Revelation 21 was not the first heaven and earth, where we now live. That was gone. Creation itself, which has been suffering the torment of sin and evil with us, gets to enjoy a dramatic makeover too. Romans 8 says the entirety of creation was subjected to futility after the fall of man, and has been groaning as in the pains of childbirth until now. It is debated whether this new heaven and new earth will be a renovation of the old, or a replacement of it, but whatever path God chooses, it will be brand new.

Psalm 19:1 says, "The heavens declare the glory of God, the skies proclaim the work of his hands." Romans 1 teaches that creation reveals God's invisible qualities, his eternal power, and divine nature, and makes them clearly seen. We all identify with that when we spend time on Mt Rainier, or on Hurricane Ridge overlooking the ocean, or a million other places on earth - we see and sense the grandeur of God.

Just wait till He gets going!

This is the crescendo of the redemptive story. It will be a new creation that reveals even more about God. The Bible says our eyes have not seen nor have our minds conceived what God has prepared for those who love Him. This new creation will be beautiful, we will be beautiful, and all things will be beautifully new. We will receive a new body and a new name, sing a new song, drink new wine, and live in the new Jerusalem. It is the first time that we will, in a state of immortality, be in the very presence of God, face to face. Sin and death will be no more and we will be a community completely free of evil, sin, death, and darkness. What a glorious, glorious day, that will be!

> "See what great love the Father has lavished on us, that we should be called children of God! That is what we are! The reason the world does not know us is that it did not know him. Dear friends, now we are children of God, and what we will be has not yet been made known. But we know that when Christ appears, we shall be like him, for we shall see him as he is. All who have this hope in Him purify themselves, just as He is pure." **- 1 John 3:1-3**

PRAYER

Great God, in whom, for whom, and through whom all things exist. Everything you have made is connected to you and reveals you. In your grace, you will make all things new and introduce all of redeemed creation into an eternal home. I thank you for your grace and I eagerly await an amazing eternity with you. As I hope in you, help me to purify myself, just as you are pure. Amen.

REFLECTION QUESTIONS

» What is the most beautiful place on earth that you have ever seen? What does it reveal about God?
» What is one thing you hope will be true about your experience in Heaven?
» "We will be like Him for we will see Him as He is" - let your imagination play with that scene for a minute or two. Thank God for this blessed Hope.
» Practice the memory verse.

_____

_____

_____

_____

_____

_____

_____

_____

_____

_____

_____

_____

_____

CONVERSATION 8 DISCUSSION
HOW IS IT ALL GOING TO END?

Truth #36 Christ will Return Again, in Victory
Truth #37 Every Person Will Give an Account to God
Truth #38 Hell is the Eternal Home for Those who Reject God
Truth #39 Heaven is Prepared for The Redeemed
Truth #40 There Will be a New Heaven and a new Earth

Gather with your Pursuit Group and have the following discussion:

» Take turns reciting this Week's memory verse: Revelation 21:1-2
» Are you eager for the return of Jesus? Why or why not?
» How does knowing the war is already won help you choose peace in the middle of your current battle? Or does it?
» Are you personally able to live in perpetual peace about the day of judgment? Why or why not?
» What is the most difficult part of the concept of eternal punishment for you to get your arms around?
» If it is not about the deeds we have done, why are our deeds being recorded in God's books? (hint: see Truth #13)
» Is the idea of Hell difficult for you? Why or why not?
» Who ends up in Hell?
» Why is it possible to know for certain that your eternal destiny is Heaven?
» What do you most anticipate about Heaven? What will be the best part?
» If you get to ask God one question when you first arrive in Heaven, what will you ask?
» What is the most beautiful place on earth you've ever been? Where is one place you've never been that you would you like to visit?
» What is one thing you hope will be true about your experience in Heaven?
» How has the Pursuit gone for you? How would you summarize your experience?
» Check out the Next Steps page and share what you plan to do next.
» Share prayer requests and current life issues with one another.
» Pray for each other.

WHAT IS NEXT?

Thank you for going on *The Pursuit* with us! I am so grateful for your sacrifice of time, energy, and community. It is my prayer that in this process you have found a deeper connection to Christ and a stronger faith, not to mention a few deeper relationships with your Pursuit Partners.

Now is the time to consider what is next in your own spiritual formation. Below are some suggestions to consider. Place a check next to the items you plan to pursue, and list one or two of your own ideas and check those as well. Then date and sign this page and let's get started on our next steps, growing together into the people of God who glorify His name and eagerly await His return!

My Next Steps

- ☐ Continue my daily study habit with a new plan
- ☐ Continue meeting with a small group
- ☐ Be baptized in water
- ☐ Memorize a new passage of scripture weekly
- ☐ Go on a prayer and study retreat to hear from God
- ☐ Find a place to regularly serve
- ☐ Go on a missions trip
- ☐ Establish family devotion times at home
- ☐ Do a one-day Fast to hear from God
- ☐ Establish a daily prayer time
- ☐ _____
- ☐ _____
- ☐ _____
- ☐ _____

Signed: _____ Date:_____

Made in the USA
San Bernardino, CA
28 January 2019